"A heartfelt and practical guide to the application of mindfulness for approaching, resting within, and ultimately transforming one's relationship to social fears and inhibitions."

> —Zindel V. Segal, Ph.D., author of *The Mindful Way Through Depression*

"Steve Flowers has written a warm, accessible, funny, and practical book to help people use mindfulness to reduce problematic shyness. With great good humor, he also shares personal experiences, challenges, and insights that helped him overcome his own shyness. His book is a valuable contribution to the self-help literature on shyness, revealing how shyness is adaptive, how it can turn into a barrier to achieving your goals, and how it can become another passing experience that you can notice, accept, and then let go, so that it doesn't diminish your quality of life."

> —Lynne Henderson, Ph.D., faculty member at Stanford University

"*The Mindful Path Through Shyness* draws on transformative meditations and psychological wisdom. The anecdotes and guided practices provide a wonderful support, not only for those who suffer from anxiety, but for all who wish to live an openhearted and mindful life."

> —Tara Brach, Ph.D., author of *Radical Acceptance*

"*The Mindful Path Through Shyness* is a generous offering of the powerful and practical tools of mindfulness practice, specifically geared to the situation of those who are living with debilitating shyness and social anxiety disorder."

> —Sharon Salzberg, author of *Lovingkindness*

"Reader, in your hands is a beautifully crafted elucidation of the healing power of mindfulness for catalyzing a powerful, positive shift in your relationship to shyness and social anxiety. Clear, kind, and wise, it is a true call to remember the fullness that we are behind our symptoms and suffering. Eminently practical, the use of metaphor is striking and revelatory. Here's one: 'If shyness is a wilderness, mindfulness is your compass.' Steve Flowers has walked in this wilderness; he has found the trail. With tremendous care and attention, he shows us a way through."

—Saki F. Santorelli, Ed.D., MA, associate professor of medicine at the University of Massachusetts Medical School and author of *Heal Thyself*

"Shyness is more than a social inconvenience. It can be a debilitating process that keeps us from making the intimate connections with others that is biologically and psychologically necessary for our well-being. Steve Flowers uses his considerable skill and wisdom to illuminate this dilemma with the light of mindfulness practice. He presents compassionate insight and practical guidance that gently lead us into an authentic ease and confidence in our social surroundings."

—William Martin, author of *The Parent's Tao Te Ching*

the mindful path through shyness

How Mindfulness & Compassion Can Help Free You from Social Anxiety, Fear & Avoidance

STEVE FLOWERS, MFT

New Harbinger Publications, Inc.

Publisher's Note

Distributed in Canada by Raincoast Books

Copyright © 2009 by Steve Flowers
New Harbinger Publications, Inc.
5674 Shattuck Avenue
Oakland, CA 94609
www.newharbinger.com

Cover design by Amy Shoup
Text design by Michele Waters-Kermes
Acquired by Jess O'Brien;
Edited by Jasmine Star

FSC
Mixed Sources
Product group from well-managed
forests and other controlled sources

Cert no. SW-COC-002283
www.fsc.org
© 1996 Forest Stewardship Council

Library of Congress Cataloging-in-Publication Data

Flowers, Steven H.
  The mindful path through shyness : how mindfulness and compassion can help free you from social anxiety, fear, and avoidance / Steven H. Flowers.
    p. cm.
  Includes bibliographical references.
  ISBN-13: 978-1-57224-650-8 (pbk. : alk. paper)
  ISBN-10: 1-57224-650-2 (pbk. : alk. paper) 1. Bashfulness. 2. Social phobia. 3. Fear. I. Title.
  BF575.B3F55 2009
  158.2--dc22
                              2009023480

11   10   09

10   9   8   7   6   5   4   3   2   1   First printing

To Mary Anne,
the love of my live

contents

Mindfulness Practices

See for Yourself Exercises

Self-Exploration Exercises

foreword

Shyness in all of its forms, including social anxiety, exacts a painful toll on us as individuals, interpersonally in relationships, and as members of larger communities. Outward appearances of shyness or behaviors of social avoidance usually reflect an inner life marked by what Steve Flowers calls "trances of fear and inadequacy." Such trances are self-sustaining through deeply entrenched habit patterns in mind and body, and they are intense. They create a profound degree of suffering for the person who is experiencing them.

And who *hasn't* felt anxiety or fear in response to a relationship or a social situation?

While some authorities note that social anxiety is the most prevalent of the various types of recognized anxiety disorders (with a lifetime prevalence as high as 13 percent), this book points out that "it is not weird to be shy." Perhaps as many as 50 percent of Americans are shy, according to some surveys.

So, it is with much appreciation and great respect for Steve Flowers and this book, and with deep compassion for all who are touched by painful shyness and anxiety, that I am happy and motivated to write this foreword. I know Steve Flowers as a friend and colleague, and as a fellow practitioner of mindfulness in the larger community of those now doing mindfulness-based stress reduction and other mindfulness-based interventions. Steve is a dedicated student of mindfulness practice and meditation, and has many years of experience doing personal meditation practice and teaching mindfulness. Moreover, whenever I have been around Steve, I have felt immediately the depth and warmth of his presence, gentleness, and great respect for others.

It is no surprise, then, that these same qualities—presence, gentleness, and respect—reach out to the reader from every page of his book. Steve has created a sensitive, mindful investigation of shyness that invites any reader very gently into the possibility of a totally new way of being. He suggests that by developing mindfulness more explicitly in your life, no matter how shy or avoidant you may feel, you can "grow through shyness" and find a life that is infinitely more satisfying and joyful. And he offers a very clear path for you to follow to explore the possibility and process of growing through shyness for yourself.

This book is accessible and easy to follow. Steve uses skillful and entertaining personal examples and revelations to guide the reader through basic concepts such as the nature of shyness and mindfulness. Along the way, he offers beautiful and detailed instructions for the actual practice of mindfulness, suggests many ways to work mindfully with thoughts and emotions associated with shyness, illuminates the importance of cultivating kindness and compassion for yourself, and illustrates the application of mindfulness and compassion to promote less fear and more happiness in relationships and social settings.

Following Steve's guidance, if you read this book carefully and actually practice the different meditations offered, you will likely find powerful healing and much insight into yourself and the true nature of shyness, anxiety, and fear.

What truths could help you "grow through anxiety"? *Anxiety and fear are not an identity, and they are not permanent. They will not destroy you, and you already have what you need to learn a better way to manage them.*

By developing your capacity to be mindful—which can happen if you practice the meditations in this book—you will naturally increase your capacity to spend more time in awareness (instead of being lost in habits of reacting reflexively and going on autopilot), and will inhabit the present moment more deeply and consciously. Paying more attention, on purpose, in this moment, and to your inner life, you will learn how mindfulness can lead you to a different experience and a growing understanding of—and freedom from—the previously unrecognized interplay of thoughts, emotions, and bodily sensations, including those associated with shyness and social anxiety.

Although the above statements may make some sense intuitively, many people still want to know whether there is any scientific evidence that mindfulness can help you. Current research indicates that mindfulness practice may work in a variety of ways to improve quality of life and to reduce anxiety and stress. For example, the tendency to ruminate and worry has been found to diminish in subjects practicing mindfulness, many clinical studies have reported that individuals with a variety of medical conditions report less anxiety when they practice mindfulness, and some researchers have found that the actual areas of the brain associated with greater self-reports of well-being are more active in people who practice mindfulness.

But, ultimately, it is you and only you who can say if practicing mindfulness has helped you, and in what ways. As Steve points out repeatedly in this book, mindfulness is to be experienced, and is perhaps best regarded as a way to approach life, not as merely a technique or fix for a problem. To find out if this is true, or even what it actually means, you will just have to do it—practice mindfulness—and see for yourself!

This book can help you discover whether mindfulness can help you find a richer and happier life. I urge you to keep the book close and enjoy reading it and practicing with it. Treating it as a good friend, you might return to it often, savoring the language, accepting the invitations for greater awareness, and allowing yourself to experience mindfulness and compassion directly by doing the practices, over and over again.

No matter how much doubt you are feeling now or how much anxiety may be upsetting you, you can take refuge in the fact that you are not the first to feel those things, or to feel stuck in them. The practices in this book and the wisdom generated by the practices of mindfulness have been the vehicle for countless others to change their relationship to fear and anxiety and to discover a new life and new possibilities for living.

I hope you will take this opportunity to discover for yourself the power of mindfulness. May your own life be filled with ease and peace as a result, and may that peace benefit countless others and our world.

—Jeffrey Brantley, MD, DFAPA
   director, Mindfulness-Based Stress Reduction Program
   Duke Integrative Medicine
   author, *Calming Your Anxious Mind* and coauthor
   with Wendy Millstine of the Five Good Minutes series
   and *Daily Meditations for Calming Your Anxious Mind*

acknowledgments

As I read over this book, I hear the echoes of many voices that are not my own and feel so much gratitude for the generosity, wisdom, and beauty of the hundreds of friends and teachers who fill its pages, as well as my heart. I can name only a few of them here.

My heartfelt love and gratitude go out to my dear friend Bob Stahl, who not only embodies compassion and wisdom, but gives freely of himself to everyone fortunate enough to know him; to Jon Kabat-Zinn, whose wisdom and generosity of spirit are a light in the world; and to Saki Santorelli, for his many gifts of kindness, clarity, and love.

I have the greatest appreciation for my skillful and patient editors at New Harbinger—Jasmine Star and Jess Beebe—who contributed so much goodwill, wise guidance, and clarity to the creation of this book; Wendy Millstine, whose initiative in acquiring this book set the whole great wheel in motion: and Jess O'Brien, whose editorial midwifery saw this book through from its earliest conception to its completion in print.

I am deeply grateful to all of the people who gave so generously of their time to read and reread the drafts of this book and offer their reflections and support, especially Bob Stahl, Lynne Henderson, Kristy Lin Billuni, Marcia Tarabini, Howard Blumenfeld, Florence Meyers, Melissa Blacker, Beth Roth, Jeffrey Brantley, and Susan Kaiser Greenland. I also wish to thank Sharon Salzberg, Tara Brach, Daniel Siegel, Zindel Segal, Bill Martin, and Gregory Kramer for their generosity of spirit and willingness to read my work and offer their support.

Of all those that have made this book possible, my wife Mary has given me the most. She has not only supported me with her wisdom, patience, and tolerance, but has taught me so much of what love is through her own loving kindness, forgiveness, and compassion, that I might dare to share these gifts of the heart with others. To her I owe the heart of this book.

introduction: approaching a mindful path

And the day came when the risk it took to remain tight inside the bud was more painful than the risk it took to blossom.

—Anaïs Nin

Being the son of a military pilot, I was often the new kid at many different schools in different neighborhoods, states, and even countries. I never seemed to fit in. It didn't help to have a last name like Flowers and to be so fair and thin, with a head of blond curls that my mother loved and therefore insisted on. It was like someone had painted a target on my back and every new school brought another bully to tease me. "Flower girl! Weeds! Pansy!" My name seemed like a curse. One particularly mean and huge sixth-grader would regularly chase me home when I was in fifth grade. I became a fast runner and could outrun the other kids, but I could never outrun the specter of my own fearfulness or my shame for being such a coward. And the faster and farther I ran, the more my anxious identity stuck to me.

Because of my fear and shame, I became increasingly disconnected from other kids and feared their judgments as much as I feared the bullies. Avoiding the other kids made me feel safer, but I couldn't escape from the shaming words and feelings in my inner world.

As a boy, I learned why people use the phrase "painfully shy." It's painful to feel anxious and unsafe in the world, and to think there's something wrong with you. You don't want others to see this private pain because then they too will think there's something wrong with you. You can end up hiding how you feel from everyone and living in a world in which no one really knows you. My family eventually moved to Japan and I left that bully on the other side of the world, but my sense of inadequacy and social anxiety followed me everywhere. I kept these feelings of inadequacy and shame for a long time. In fact, they stayed with me into adulthood as I made avoiding other people a way of life.

If you identify as being shy or socially anxious, you can probably relate to some of these experiences. Fearing the judgments and rejection of others, you avoid people and find yourself principally in a relationship with your own thoughts and feelings. Unfortunately, often this isn't such a great relationship. In fact, you've probably noticed that you can say critical things to yourself that you would never say to anyone else—or tolerate from anyone else, for that matter. It's a predicament. You can't outrun your own thoughts and feelings, so your meanest critic can follow you anywhere and often does.

As you read this, you may recognize an important and fundamental truth: that the pain of shyness and social anxiety is not only created by these self-critical thoughts and feelings, it's exacerbated into personal suffering by our efforts to avoid or escape from these thoughts and feelings.

It's only natural that you would try to use the same escape and avoidance strategy with thoughts and feelings that you've used with external threats; it's what most people do. Unfortunately, the very effort to escape thoughts, or even suppress or control them, usually intensifies them (Gross and Levenson 1997; Purdon 1999). As a result, this way of trying to deal with mental and emotional difficulties can lead to entrenched patterns that create a confusing mess, and more suffering in our lives.

Suppose you don't have to try to avoid or control painful thoughts and feelings to reduce their power and influence in your life. What if there's a way to let them be, and instead put your energy into what you value in life? What if you don't have to seek out personality flaws and fix them in order to have fulfilling interpersonal relationships? What if being flawed has nothing to do with deep and satisfying relationships with other people after all? (You've got to know it doesn't, otherwise satisfying relationships would be impossible for everyone.) In this book, I'll introduce you to how a powerful internal resource known as mindfulness can help you come into a healthier relationship with painful thoughts and feelings, and help you come home to being who and where you are.

how can mindfulness help shyness?

Mindfulness is the awareness that grows from being present in the unfolding moments of our lives without judging or trying to change anything that we experience. It's a friendly and curious awareness that we all have, though we may not experience it very often because we are so rarely present with and accepting of things as they are. Problematic shyness and social anxiety are inherently self-critical and rejecting, whereas the nature of mindful awareness is compassionate and accepting. Learning to look at yourself with awareness rather than criticism is an enormous change that will allow you to begin to see the habits of mind and behavior that exacerbate the pain of shyness. This new awareness can loosen the grip of these old habits and reduce their power to influence you.

The principal work of a mindfulness-based approach to working with shyness is therefore to grow in awareness and self-compassion and learn how to bring this awareness into your life whenever you can. I want to underscore an important distinction: the work isn't to get rid of shyness or change any of your thoughts and feelings; it's about cultivating compassionate awareness. Shyness can become just another facet of the many aspects of yourself. You can quit struggling with it and just let it be, and instead attend to the facets of yourself that you would like to see grow.

The mindfulness-based approaches you'll be introduced to here have been demonstrated to be effective in reducing anxiety and depression (Orsillo and Roemer 2005). In the chapters ahead, I'll discuss some of this research, as it can help you understand the value of mindfulness and provide some support for your own investment in practice. However, the kind of intellectual understanding you gain from reading about the benefits of mindfulness won't provide the resources you need

3

to free yourself from the suffering of shyness. You need to *practice* mindfulness to reap these benefits. The key to healing along a mindful path is awareness—actually experiencing awareness, not thinking about, reading about, or studying it. In a conversation I had with meditation teacher Larry Rosenberg a few years ago, he told me, "I don't need research to know that meditation is good for me." Larry has a way of cutting to the chase about things like this. In the pages that follow, you'll have a chance to experience and see this for yourself.

Identifying yourself as shy doesn't mean there's something wrong with you. You can feel shy and also be happy and deeply connected with other people. By becoming more mindful of how you create suffering with your way of relating to shyness, you can stop creating suffering and realize your highest values. The mental and behavioral habits of shyness that cause suffering operate unconsciously and automatically, whereas the intentions of mindfulness are conscious and deliberate. As you make the shift from unconscious to conscious and from reacting to responding, your self-concept and habits of mind will seem less substantial and locked in stone.

Any one of us can become identified with some concept of who we are and then perpetuate this self-concept with our thoughts and actions. We may identify with a profession, a family or social role, a particular personality trait like shyness, or any number of other aspects of ourselves. Once we arrive at this self-concept, we tend to remain there and believe that's who we are. We then seek to prove our self-concepts in everything we do and rarely notice anything to the contrary. For example, if you're giving a presentation, you can prove to yourself that no one likes it by focusing on the faces in the audience that are frowning and ignoring those that are smiling or captivated.

As long as you identify with the thoughts, emotions, and behaviors related to shyness or social anxiety, you'll remain locked into a shy and anxious identity and come to think this is who you are. But by centering yourself in mindful awareness, you'll come to see that this identity is just a collection of mental habits and therefore only represents those habits. By observing these mental and emotional habits and letting them be, you become more than your constructed identity; you become the awareness that is observing that constructed identity with compassion and acceptance. You are no longer centered within that identity or defined by it.

4

This book is a synthesis of mainstream psychology, medical research, and a meditation practice called mindfulness meditation. This is a joining of scientific knowledge gained from empirical research with the wisdom discovered by means of the "inner research" of meditation. More specifically, I'll guide you on a healing path that's a union of the practices and attitudes of mindfulness meditation with key principles and tools from cognitive behavioral therapy (CBT).

CBT emphasizes how our ways of thinking about and reacting to things create much of the suffering in our lives and offers techniques to change those maladaptive thoughts. A mindfulness-based approach to healing also recognizes the power of thoughts to shape our lives, but it attends to thoughts with acceptance and compassion and works with them by exploring them in awareness. It isn't always necessary to try to change thoughts if you recognize that you aren't defined by them. Mindfulness is a practice of investigation that enables you to become more sensitive and attentive to thoughts and emotions from a center of awareness that is separate from them and therefore able to witness them as discrete events. Mindfulness practices enable you to separate yourself from your thoughts, and this alone is an extremely powerful skill for reducing the power and influence of difficult thoughts and emotions. As you learn to trust your compassionate observer self, you can return to it more often and more easily. In time, it will feel more like home than like a new vantage point.

The essential components of mindfulness are antithetical to the components of shyness that create suffering:

- As mindfulness is nonjudging, you can be accepting of yourself rather than self-critical.

- As mindfulness is a moment-to-moment, here-and-now awareness, you can actually be here rather than in some imagined future you feel anxious about.

- As mindfulness is turning toward and being with, you can stop avoiding the thoughts and feelings that scare you and stop generating the self-criticism and shame that can be fueled by avoidance.

- As mindfulness is compassionate and openhearted aware-ness, you can extend compassion to yourself rather than condemnation.

- As mindfulness is awakening to the fullness of being, you can stop identifying with a false and limiting sense of self.

- As mindfulness is nonjudging and compassionate, you can free yourself from the prison of self-consciousness and extend the same generosity of spirit to others that you extend to yourself.

Mindfulness has no agenda. It's a way of being rather than a means to an end. Shifting into the perspective of mindful awareness, you simply are where you are, as you are. You can discover a place here, within yourself, that isn't governed by the nagging critic and the ever-striving but always insufficient performer in your head. When centered in this place of wholeness, you can make mindful choices and experience greater freedom.

However, do be aware that these benefits don't come overnight or all at once; they are generally discovered along the way rather than achieved. It can take a long time to discover your wholeness and completeness, even though it's been your essential nature all along. Be patient. There is much to be discovered. In fact, the mindful path is really each moment and every step you take along the way.

how to best use this book

Please invest yourself in the exercises and practices in this book. As mentioned above, you can't build awareness by reading about awareness; you have to actually *practice* awareness. I once got lost in a wilderness area with my wife even though I had brought a compass and topographical map with me. Knowing nothing about wilderness orienteering, I smugly assured myself and my wife that these were all I needed. I soon discovered these tools are useless unless you plot your course with them all along. I had never learned that the only way to avoid getting lost is to stay found.

Trying to get back to our camp after a long hike one evening, we were both feeling extremely anxious as we went by the same landmark the third time (actually, my wife was getting pretty pissed off). Fortunately, we stopped at that point and discovered that we had another compass to get our bearings with: by some miracle, we quieted down for a few moments and heard the distant murmur of a creek—the creek we had hiked in on. We had found our way home by shifting out of the anxious clamoring of our thoughts and into the immediacy of our senses.

When you stop to actually be where you are, you can make these types of liberating discoveries anywhere, anytime. You might consider your experience of shyness as a wilderness of sorts—an unmapped territory that's unique to you. Finding your way out will require your own mindful awareness. No one else can walk this path for you. You must choose to be present so that you can stay found.

Consider this book as a map. Like the one that I brought with me on my trip in the wilderness, it can help you plot your course. However, you will find your way to a place where you feel safe and free from anxiety only if you actually practice mindful awareness of yourself and your surroundings using the exercises and practices in the book and noting your progress along the way. A good way to do this is by writing a little about your experiences in a shyness journal. Please buy a special journal and use it to contemplate and record your thoughts, feelings, and insights along this journey.

a mindful compass

Sometimes we just show up—we find ourselves being mindful without an explicit intention to do so. It's usually surprising when this happens. We accidentally slip out of the world of our thoughts and suddenly see, hear, and discover things we weren't noticing before. These experiences may not always be accessible entirely by choice, but they can be promoted by mindfulness practices. Mindfulness involves inclining ourselves or leaning into the immediacy of our moment-to-moment experience rather than into mental commentaries or interpretations about what's happening now. It requires a certain amount of faith that being fully present is beneficial and a certain amount of intention to return to the present moment when you notice you've left it. Your awareness will help you see and hear things more vividly and help you recognize how your thoughts and emotions are influencing your experience of the here and now. Consider this as consulting your mindful compass—a compass that has always been with you, even if obscured by thoughts, feelings, and avoidant behaviors.

Let's establish that there are four primary readings to take on this compass: your thoughts, emotions, sensations, and behaviors. When you consult this compass, you might simply acknowledge what you're experiencing and label it as pleasant, unpleasant, or neutral. It's easy to see how this applies to thoughts, emotions, and sensations, but what about behavior? Extending compassion to yourself or others is a pleasant behavior, and criticizing yourself or others is generally unpleasant. Let's also say that there's a little dial on this compass you can use to set your primary heading. Set it to self-compassion. This may not be the direction you've traveled so far, but if your usual approach were working, you wouldn't be reading this book. Self-compassion will give you a greater ease of being in the world, particularly in the scary and often complicated world of interpersonal relationships.

Because mindfulness enables you to see where you are in any given moment, it can help you choose what direction you need to take. Much of the work we'll do together in this book will help you learn to read and follow this simple but profoundly helpful compass through problematic shyness and social anxiety and beyond.

Though the idea of attending to painful thoughts and feelings may be daunting, your journey into mindfulness will also reveal much that is right with you and the world and bring you to a place of peace, well-being, and greater lightness of spirit. Mindfulness can reveal that you are whole and complete right now, just as you are, and that you can be happy in this life, just as it is.

In part 1 of this book, I'll provide a mindful perspective on shyness and social anxiety. We'll explore what problematic shyness is and the ways we construct it and perpetuate it. I'll also provide an introduction to mindfulness and compassion and show you how these practices can aid in healing and help you find your way to a place where you are no longer driven by habits of escape and avoidance. Finally, you'll also find a certain amount of factual information in this section that I need to cover to help you better understand the rest of the book.

In part 2, you will develop mindfulness and self-awareness through meditation and other awareness practices. You'll also learn how embracing the nonverbal world will deepen your understanding of yourself and the expression of your true nature. Knowing and expressing yourself in this way will help reduce the pain of shyness and social anxiety in your life.

In part 3, you'll further deepen your mindfulness practice and bring it to bear on working with the thoughts, emotions, and behaviors that create and perpetuate difficulties with shyness. Some of the exercises will help you recognize how you may have become more entrenched in unhealthy mental states, and you'll learn mindfulness practices that will help you free yourself from this entrenchment. You'll learn that you aren't your thoughts, that you can welcome your emotions without being consumed or controlled by them, and that freedom from some of of the most vexing problems of shyness often lies in turning toward those emotions and experience you'd rather avoid.

In part 4, you'll learn how to apply the skills you've learned in your personal practice of mindfulness and compassion in your relationships with others. Compassion will allow you to experience your similarities to others and foster a sense of connectedness. This in turn will allow you to continue to grow in mindfulness, and as you become more connected to the wholeness of the world around you, you'll find you also develop an even deeper sense of your own wholeness.

If you read this book without doing the mindfulness practices I offer, you'll still gain a greater understanding of the nature of shyness and what mindfulness is, but you may not make much progress on the problems that shyness brings. It would be like reading a menu but not eating the meal. Please take the time to savor this meal; doing so will make your entire life more of a feast.

the mindful path through shyness program

As we begin this journey through shyness together, I want to let you know about the eight-week Mindful Path Through Shyness Program (MPTS) and a workbook that will enable you to get the most out of this book to reduce shyness and social anxiety in your life. Please go to www.mindfullivingprograms.com and download the free MPTS Program and its accompanying workbook. You'll also find on this site numerous additional resources for your ongoing work with shyness and social anxiety; including recorded media, mindfulness retreats, and links where you may practice interpersonal mindfulness skills with others.

Before we begin the first chapter, I want you to have the means to bring mindfulness into all that you read and do with this book. From time to time you may read something that rings true or seems important to you. These would be good times to stop and feel your breathing for a few minutes. With that in mind, please take a few moments to pause from your reading and experience mindful breathing with the following practice.

mindfulness practice:
Mindful Breathing

You are always breathing, so you can practice mindfulness of your breath anywhere, anytime. This is a powerful and convenient way to become present wherever you go and in whatever you do. We'll explore a variety of mindfulness practices later in the book, but for now I'd like you to experience mindfulness with as much clarity as possible, so I've kept this first exercise simple and straightforward. After you read these instructions, please close your eyes and invest five minutes or so in just being present with your breath.

Sitting comfortably where you are right now, bring your body into a posture that is upright and supported, with a sense of balance and dignity. See if you can align your head, neck, and body in a way that is neither too rigid nor too relaxed, but somewhere in between. The intention is to be wakeful and alert, yet not tense; at ease, but not drifting off to sleep.

Bring attention to your breathing, focusing on your belly and noticing the sensation of your breath coming and going. If you like, place a hand on your belly to feel this movement. Notice how your belly rises as you inhale and descends again as you exhale. This is because we breathe by way of the diaphragm, a muscle that expands downward in the belly as we breathe in, causing the belly to rise. Make the rising and falling of your belly the center of your attention and simply let your breath come and go as it will, in its own way and with its own pace. Your breath knows how to breathe you, and you can let it do what it does without trying to change it in any way. If your mind wanders from your breath, you may return to it again by feeling your belly's movement. Use these sensations of your breath as your way to be present, here and now, in each successive moment for at least the next five minutes, and longer if you like.

As you come to the end of this practice, please sit with the following questions for a couple of minutes: What brings you here to work with shyness and social anxiety? What is the vision you have of yourself and your life if you were free from fear, anxiety, and avoidance?

Notes to Yourself

Throughout this book, I'll invite you to pause and write notes to yourself. Please use these times to pause for a few minutes and practice mindful breathing, then write in your shyness journal for a few minutes on the topic at hand. For now, write a little on the questions above and on what you experienced during your mindful breathing practice. After you finish writing, put your journal down, once again close your eyes, and spend a couple more minutes with the rising and falling of your belly as you breathe. Consider this felt sense of your breath in your belly as your way to orient yourself into the here and now anytime you like. Consider this place as home.

PART I

starting from where you are

Until one is committed, there is hesitancy, the chance to draw back, always ineffectiveness. Concerning all acts of initiative (and creation), there is one elementary truth, the ignorance of which kills countless ideas and splendid plans: that the moment one definitely commits oneself, then providence moves too. All sorts of things occur to help one that would never otherwise have occurred. A whole stream of events issues from the decision, raising in one's favor all manner of unforeseen incidents and meetings and material assistance, which no man could have dreamed would have come his way. Whatever you can do, or dream you can do, begin it. Boldness has genius, power, and magic in it. Begin it now.

—William Hutchinson Murray,
from *The Scottish Himalayan
Expedition*

the nature of shyness

The mind is its own place, and in itself can make a Heaven of hell, a hell of Heaven.

—John Milton

Life is fraught with peril. From our very first breath, all of us are sensitive and vulnerable and cannot avoid illness, injury, and death. We can't survive without one another, yet we also can't avoid being separated from one another. We will hurt and be hurt by one another in many ways. The experience of shyness involves being exquisitely sensitive to interpersonal peril and seeking to protect yourself from the pain inherent in relationships.

Given that you experience a lot of shyness, one of the ways you may have chosen to protect yourself is by avoiding significant interpersonal relationships altogether. This is logical as it prevents a great deal of pain and angst, and in the short run it works—you do feel less anxious. The problem is that you're then stuck with all of the difficulties that come with not having significant relationships, like loneliness. This is a particularly painful problem when you feel angry and critical, and with no one else to talk with, you may end up judging and blaming yourself. Unfortunately, people with shyness can often spend a lot of time doing just that.

There's a particular kind of suffering you experience with shyness yet you want the things that successful relationships can bring, like loving and being loved, a sense of belonging, or even advancing in your career. The very thing you want makes you feel anxious. The purpose of this book is to help with this kind of suffering.

Shyness is made up of characteristic thoughts, emotions, sensations, and behaviors that are entirely malleable and within your power to change. In this chapter, we'll explore how various thoughts, feelings, and behaviors come together to create shyness.

our lives are made of patterns

We create habitual patterns of behavior in our lives and then live in them. Some we create consciously, like a morning jog, but most of our patterns are formed unconsciously by repeating certain thoughts, feelings, and actions so often that we become stuck in them. Research has shown that problematic shyness has core components of self-blame, private self-consciousness, shame, and resentment (Henderson, Zimbardo, and Carducci 2001). These habits of mind operate automatically and often unconsciously, below the threshold of awareness. They are something we do, not something we are, and once created and in place, they are generally predictable and arise instantly on cue.

Imagine going into a restaurant at lunch intending to sit and eat, but a coworker sees you enter and jumps up to invite you to join him and three others for lunch. You immediately feel nervous, smile, and thank him for the invitation but make up an excuse, telling him you just came in for some takeout. You flee to the takeout counter. You didn't plan this reaction to an unexpected invitation; it came automatically. As you leave the restaurant, you feel a flood of relief, but you also feel frustrated and self-critical. You really don't want to end up eating lunch in your car, and you may wonder what's wrong with you and why you can't be more sociable.

As a person struggling with shyness, you have your own unique blend of mental and emotional habits that forms and perpetuates your individual shyness pattern. The pattern is automatic and hard to control and can create much pain and suffering in your life. As in the movie *Groundhog Day*, we tend to remain stuck in unexamined ways of doing things, repeating the same pattern day after day. You're likely to remain stuck until you can find a perspective that allows you to explore and understand your mental and emotional patterns without being controlled by them.

It's important to get beyond your problematic shyness patterns so that they don't automatically define and limit your life. You need to begin looking at the patterns themselves and trying to understand how they work. Are they rigid or flexible, changing or unchanging? How well do they serve you? How are those patterns created by your thoughts and emotions, and how do they drive what you do?

We usually don't look deeply into these patterns or understand them well. In fact, we're usually swept along in the same deeply ingrained habits we developed as very young children. But we do have the ability to examine these things and recognize how we're repeating old and sometimes painful patterns, and this is where mindfulness is so valuable. The more we look into our life patterns, the more we can take them off automatic pilot. There are many ways to respond to any given situation. Mindfulness can help you find new responses to old triggers so that you can live more in accordance with your highest values.

One way to arrive at a more deliberate, mindful response is to pause at a trigger point, at least for a moment or two, before you do anything at all. Within that mindful pause, you may notice that you can respond rather than react to the situation. In the example above, you might pause and reflect for a moment before responding to your coworker's invitation to have lunch together. You may still decide you don't want to join the group, but now this decision came from a choice, rather than a knee-jerk reaction. It's perfectly alright to sit alone to eat if that's what you want to do, but it's also perfectly alright to sit with your coworkers even if you do feel uncomfortable.

By bringing mindful awareness to your cognitive and emotional states, you can illuminate them, thereby allowing you to better regulate your attention and emotions (Teasdale, Segal, and Williams 1995).

shyness and suffering

Shyness is one thing, and suffering is another. Shyness doesn't cause suffering, but how you perceive it and react to it certainly can. If you can learn to look deeply into your shyness pattern, you may discover what you're doing within it that creates suffering. While each person's story and pattern are unique, there are often three principal components in the shyness pattern that create a lot of difficulty in the lives of folks who identify as shy: anticipating the future, imagining the worst, and avoidance. When you anticipate future social events and imagine the worst, you suffer. If you decide to avoid everything that makes you feel anxious, you suffer. If you've grown to hate your shyness or hate yourself for feeling shy, you suffer. If you've decided that you don't ever want to feel anxious or afraid again, you suffer. When you're stuck in a shyness pattern, *aversion* (the automatic urge to escape or avoid anything uncomfortable or repugnant) can create much suffering in your life.

If you look into your shyness pattern, you'll probably find these components, in some form or fashion. For example, imagining the worst might show up as a pessimistic attitude about the outcome of an event, or it might be a way of thinking negatively about yourself or others. Aversion may take the shape of some kind of control strategy, like asking questions and acting like a very interested listener, or ducking into a store to avoid an acquaintance on the street. As you explore the components of your shyness pattern in this book, you'll start to see what you're doing to keep it going as you closely examine your anticipations, judgments, and aversions. By bringing increased awareness into your way of doing things, you'll find the places where you do have a choice about what you do. The intention is to take your life off of automatic pilot.

What Is Shyness?

If you're reading this book, you know the experience of shyness intimately and don't need concepts to describe it. You can feel it in your gut and your hands and your heart. But we need words and concepts to talk about it. Let's start with a definition. Shyness is a human temperament often described in terms of personality traits that many regard as positive, like modesty and being quiet and demure. But some aspects of shyness aren't positive, and they create what I'll refer to as problematic shyness. These aspects include feelings of being unsafe in interpersonal relationships and feelings of social anxiety, which lead to protective behaviors.

People with problematic shyness have thoughts and emotions that are self-critical and self-absorbed. Trying to conceal those fears and perceived inadequacies can lead you to enclose yourself in a private self-consciousness, and although this enclosure is meant to protect, it actually imprisons.

Shyness can be experienced at various levels of intensity, ranging from an uncomfortable but tolerable tension to a disabling emotional condition that seriously interferes with life. At one end of the spectrum, shyness is a normal human temperament, and at the other end it's a painful form of social anxiety. When you're caught in the spell of shyness, you may be excessively focused on yourself in some social situations (situational shyness) or most social situations (generalized shyness).

Shyness is often confused with introversion, but introverts don't necessarily shy. Rather, introverts draw energy from internal resources (whereas extroverts draw energy from external resources). Introverts prefer solitary rather than social activities because that's satisfying for them; people who feel shy, on the other hand, choose solitary activities out of fear or anxiety. Both introverts or extroverts can feel shy.

I've mentioned that shyness is made up of characteristic thoughts, emotions, sensations, and behaviors. Since awareness of your existing patterns is the first step to changing them, let's take a look at how shyness typically manifests in each of these realms.

Thoughts. People dealing with shyness often think about themselves so much that those thoughts color much of what they do. These thoughts are self-focused, self-critical, and worrisome and can lead to brooding (a pattern called *rumination* in the parlance of psychology). In addition, these thoughts are generally future oriented, inflexible, automatic, and habitual. They also include storytelling—usually telling stories about oneself to oneself. Shyness also tends to lead people to engage in projection, imagining their thoughts and self-judgments in other peoples' heads.

Emotions. Folks who feel shy generally don't want anybody to see their emotions, so they often hide them, which tends to increase feelings of anxiety, fear, guilt, shame, depression, resentment, and loneliness. We all need a safe place to feel our emotions and share them with others, but for people who feel shy, the guiding principle is to avoid displays of emotion.

Sensations. The sensations and physical expressions that arise with problematic shyness are usually unwanted and embarrassing, and are therefore certain to appear when you don't want them to. People who feel shy may betray their nervousness to others in the form of trembling hands, twitching eyelids, sweating, and blushing. Other typical sensations include cold hands or feet, rapid heartbeat, nausea, dry mouth, and tension.

Behaviors. Shyness behaviors are all variations on a theme: avoid or escape. People may fidget and fuss and twirl their hair a lot before they make it out the door, and it's not unusual to drink too much. Feeling shy often means being well practiced in many different forms of avoidance.

Prevalence of Shyness

Just in case you've ever wondered, let's acknowledge that it's actually not weird to feel shy. In fact, recent surveys indicate that 50 percent or more of the general population in the United States identifies as shy (Henderson 2009; Henderson, Zimbardo, and Carducci 2001). According to the *The Book of Lists* (Wallenchinsky and Wallace 2005), the greatest human fear is public speaking, while the fear of death is our fourth greatest fear. As the comedian Jerry Seinfeld has observed, the average person at a funeral would rather be in the casket than doing the eulogy.

What Is Social Anxiety Disorder?

Social anxiety disorder, also called social phobia, is an intense fear or even terror of humiliation or embarrassment in relation to groups of people. It's very difficult to overcome and can be very disabling. For this reason, social phobia is substantially different from shyness and is classified as a mental health disorder in the *Diagnostic and Statistical Manual of Mental Disorders* (American Psychiatric Association 2004).

Do You Have Social Phobia?

According to the *Diagnostic and Statistical Manual of Mental Disorders* (American Psychiatric Association 2004), if you answer yes to three or more of the following questions and your symptoms aren't caused by medications, substance abuse, or another emotional or medical disorder, you may have social phobia:

1. Are you afraid of being in certain situations, such as socializing with or performing in groups of people who are unfamiliar to you, because you fear doing or saying something that will be embarrassing to you?

2. Do you experience symptoms of anxiety in these situations, such as rapid heartbeat, sweating, confusion, diarrhea, or, in severe cases, panic?

3. Do you believe this fear is unreasonable and excessive?

4. Do you avoid these situations whenever possible or endure them with intense anxiety and distress?

5. Do these problems seriously interfere with your social or occupational life or academic functioning? Do you feel distressed about having these problems?

Social phobia has many of the same components as shyness in terms of thoughts, emotions, sensations, and behaviors, but they're experienced much more intensely and involve feeling considerably more fear and anxiety in relation to socializing and performing in front of groups of people. As with shyness, there is *situational social phobia* (social or performance anxiety in limited situations, such as only when giving a presentation in front of colleagues at work) and *generalized social phobia* (social or performance anxiety in common situations, like eating at restaurants or meeting new people). Social phobia is extremely prevalent in the United States, affecting up to 13 percent of the population (Barlow 2002). This makes it the most common of all the anxiety disorders and the third most common mental health disorder.

Because the same components that create suffering in shyness also create suffering in social phobia, they can be addressed and significantly reduced by the approaches in this book. Please keep in mind, however, that if you aren't making progress with the problematic aspects of shyness and social anxiety, or if issues come up for you in the course of your work in this book that are persistently so distressing that you'd like more personal assistance, it would be a good idea to find a therapist you'd feel comfortable working with. Sometimes when anxiety is extremely intense or disabling, particularly if it's related to trauma, it's best to consult with a mental health professional who can assist you in your healing process. Meditation is not a substitute for therapy when therapy is called for. In the Resources section, you'll find contact information for some organization that might help you find a qualified therapist.

name-calling

Though words and labels such as "shy" and "social phobia" can be useful and even welcome sometimes, they can also be imprisoning if we identify ourselves or others with these labels. It's important to remember that these are just words or, at best, concepts, and not the whole of who you are. Words and concepts get in the way of direct experience of our moment-to-moment lives (something we'll explore at length in chapter 4).

Words are simply necessary units of the thought and communication process; they are never the stuff of immediate experience itself. The problem is that we become stuck in these abstractions and view the world and our experiences through this lens, rather than directly. Living in the world of labeling, and particularly judgmental labeling, can be a vicious habit. We can end up living in our own sometimes cruel mental constructs of reality and hardly notice anything else.

Another aspect of labeling to bear in mind is that a label may be accurate at one point in time but entirely inaccurate later. Everything is impermanent and always changing. When I was a boy, having a name like Flowers was a curse, but when I was a teenager in the 1960s it seemed like a blessing. At one time in my life I felt extremely shy, but at this point I no longer feel shy. I'm not unique in this; in surveys, nearly 40 percent of people who once considered themselves shy said they no longer felt shy (Henderson and Zimbardo 1998). We are all always changing.

Unfortunately, once you identify yourself with a label, you can actually come to think that this is who you are, and it can be surprisingly hard to let go of that identity. Identifying yourself as a shy person or an anxious person never captures the whole truth of who you are. It's worthwhile to reframe your perspective. Consider making a shift to language along the lines of "I often feel shy" or "I'm having anxious thoughts." This is one way to let go of labels.

the difference between fear and anxiety

Fear stems from an immediate threat that you experience with your senses; for example, you turn a corner and see a large, growling dog charging toward you. Anxiety, on the other hand, stems from a mental event. For example, it may come from thinking about the possibility of a large, menacing dog around the next corner. Sometimes an element of anxiety (an internal mental event) can be triggered by an external physical event through a mechanism known as *apperception*. This happens when we perceive new experiences through the lens of unremembered past experience and then react to a relatively benign physical event as though it were a threat. Using the example above, you may experience any dog as threatening even if you can't remember a traumatic event with a dog. Despite these distinctions, it's important to note that the body doesn't distinguish between fear and anxiety. For the person with a phobia about dogs, the body responds to the thought of a charging dog just as it would an actual charging dog.

During an illness a few years ago, I experienced anaphylactic shock. My throat seized up so that I couldn't breathe, and my body surged with fear. Fortunately, the episode passed in less than a minute, but even once I could take a breath, my heart still pounded and my body trembled with the chemicals and hormones it flooded itself with to meet this life-threatening event. It took about fifteen minutes before my body began to settle down and return to its steady state.

Later that night as I was about to fall asleep, I had the thought "What if that happens while I'm asleep? I could suffocate in my sleep!" Instantly my body was shot through with the same intensity of alarm as when I couldn't breathe. My heart began to pound and I felt myself begin to breathe faster and higher in my chest. As I sat up, it occurred to me that this reaction was caused not by a real event, but by a thought about what might happen. I got up for a few minutes to reflect on what had just happened to me. I realized that earlier in the day I had been too much in shock to really feel and acknowledge what had happened to me. I could have died! My heart cracked open and I cried for the terror I had experienced. When I lay back down, I felt much more connected to my aching heart and my very tired body. My breathing had slowed and deepened, and I felt it rising and falling from somewhere deep in my belly. I followed it into sleep.

Sometimes your heart calls to you and needs you to respond to it with kindness and compassion. As you shift your attention from thoughts about the future or the past to your immediate experience of what's happening now, you may experience a great wave of sadness. However, as you find your way back into your body, and back into the present moment, you'll find that the here and now provides a refuge from the perils of imagination.

the fear body

Throughout our lives, we all have many experiences of fear and anxiety. These experiences leave memories in both the mind and the body. Over the years, they form what Jeffrey Brantley calls "the fear body" in his book *Calming Your Anxious Mind* (2007). The fear body is a kind of trance state we can live in that has its own intelligence and biochemistry and perpetuates itself through automatic habits of thought, emotion, and behavior that usually remain unexamined. Meditation teacher and author Eckhart Tolle also speaks of this concept, which he refers to as "the pain body," in his books and seminars (Tolle 2004). He teaches that the pain body is trapped life energy that can become our identity and re-create pain in our lives as long as we remain unaware of it.

Complex and intricate systems in our bodies regulate our physiological state when we're afraid, and if we're often fearful and anxious, these bodily states become habituated and form the fear body. One scientific explanation of how we may become habituated to these emotional states comes from neuroscientist and author Candace Pert. She speaks of an adaptive intelligence in the brain and body that runs all of the body systems and stimulates behavior. In her research, she's found that we become addicted to substances like marijuana and heroin because our bodies have receptor sites for these chemicals. This led to her remarkable discovery that we can also become addicted to emotional states because our bodies have receptor sites for certain chemicals (peptides) that emotions create. She calls these peptides "the molecules of emotion" and has surmised that we become habituated to emotional states like fear and anxiety and need to act out the same thoughts and emotions again and again to give the body the peptides it has become used to (Pert 1998).

The fear body can be activated by thoughts, perceptions, or memories. When it does, you're likely to identify with it completely and, in effect, become the habits of mind and behavior that comprise it. At these times, you will feel the compelling tug of the fight, flight, or freeze response. Identifying as shy, you probably know flight quite intimately and also have found yourself in freeze from time to time. The freeze reaction is an effort to not be seen, and creatures like deer and cats and folks who feel shy do this quite often when they're afraid.

Everyone has a fear body, and when it's activated, powerful chemicals and hormones are pumped into the bloodstream through what is called the sympathetic nervous system. The arousal we feel helps us deal with the threat, so it's a good thing. We can run faster, hit harder, and accomplish amazing feats of strength. We see, hear, and smell better and are more alert. The heart beats faster to provide more blood to the muscles. The blood drains from the peripheral areas of the circulatory system so that if you get injured you won't bleed as much, but as it does your hands and feet feel cold. The blood also drains from the digestive tract to serve more vital purposes, and that might cause nausea or a woozy feeling in your belly. The breath moves high into the chest and becomes shallower and faster. As you can see, this evolutionarily adaptive response also creates the sensations we experience when we become charged up with fear or anxiety.

Fortunately, our bodies also have a built-in, essentially unconscious self-calming system: the parasympathetic nervous system. It has exquisitely sensitive neural networks that immediately calm us when, say, we come upon the same coiled rope that we mistook for a snake yesterday. We don't even have to think about it; it does this automatically. This self-calming system provides what Herbert Benson, MD, has called the relaxation response (1993). If the fear body is overstimulated and has become self-perpetuating as the body craves fear-based "molecules of emotion," we can cultivate a more healthful balance by practicing mindfulness and acceptance, which promote the parasympathetic nervous system and help us calm down. Our bodies can become more accustomed to calm states than alarm states with time and practice. However, these changes don't happen overnight; our bodies and minds change with the time we invest in ourselves. Once we become fully aroused, it can still take fifteen or twenty minutes for this self-calming system to bring the body back into balance, even with practice.

Social anxiety is a normal emotional reaction that most people will experience at least occasionally. It isn't some weird anomaly that only a few have been cursed with. Like any other kind of anxiety, it actually provides us with an important service, in this case stimulating our minds and bodies to meet potential social challenges, just like fear provides an important service when we face immediate physical challenges. The fact is, if you no longer felt social anxiety, you would be just as vulnerable and at risk in this world as if you no longer felt pain or fear.

the mindful path: less about causes and more about choices

A mindfulness-based approach to shyness involves bringing an enormous amount of awareness and compassion to the your direct and immediate experience of shyness or social anxiety, rather than trying to investigate its sources in your personal history. Mindfulness attends to what's happening right now, as opposed to trying to understand what happened back then. In this book, I'll encourage you to place your attention on the bare experience of what's happening here and now, and to simply observe such things as your self-evaluation and how you interpret social interactions, rather than examining how or why you developed shyness in the first place.

Suffice it to say that shyness, like most personality traits, originates in the usual intertwined sources of genetics and life experiences. Not only is there evidence that genetics can play a role in shyness, there is also substantial research that indicates shyness can be reduced or increased by the influence of primary caregivers in early childhood and other socializing influences throughout life (Kagan 1994). Sometimes nature loads the gun and nurture pulls the trigger.

However, you don't have to know the origins of your shyness to learn how to work with it differently. The things that are important for you to know will come up on their own as you do the work of opening to and being with shy thoughts and feelings. As you engage in the mindfulness practices in this book, memories from both your recent history and your early childhood will arise and enter your awareness. Some of these will bring important revelations, and others won't. From the point of view of mindfulness, the invitation is to feel whatever memories do arise and receive and acknowledge whatever messages they offer you. You aren't looking for these memories, but they will come to you and will elicit feelings that *are* happening in the present moment and may very well help you illuminate your mindful path through shyness. Meet them with compassion and make them a conscious part of you.

What has happened to you plays only a bit part in your shyness equation; what's currently happening with you plays the leading role. This shifts your focus from how you developed shyness to how you continue it. This is where the rubber meets the road: What are you doing in your life right now to keep yourself stuck in the pain of shyness? This is an important consideration, as it casts problematic shyness as something you do rather than something you are. This means that the most troublesome components of shyness are things you can work with: thoughts, emotions, sensations, and behaviors that are impermanent, malleable, and within your personal capacity to change.

The mindful path involves becoming better acquainted with anxiety and learning how to work with it more consciously. With this shift from avoidance to acceptance, anxiety becomes more peripheral and utilitarian and less central and problematic in your personality—a part of you but not all of you. For example, when anxiety comes, you might learn to acknowledge it, label it "anxiety," investigate it for a few moments to see what it's about, then give it a lot of space and let it be as you return to the immediacy of whatever you were engaged in.

When you accept the reality and place of social anxiety in your life, you can start working with it in a more deliberate way. You can start paying better attention to your thoughts and emotions and consider what is true and not true, or known and not known. You can recognize whether what you fear is an immediate, real threat or just a catastrophic projection into the future. With this increased awareness, you'll be in a good position to learn to reset and better regulate the self-protection systems of your fear body. Through compassionate awareness and acceptance, you can take the cascade of automatic thoughts, emotions, and reactions off of automatic and begin accessing some of the self-calming and self-soothing resources of your mind and body.

mindfulness practice:
Mindful Breathing

Please pause for five or ten minutes, or as long as you like, to practice the mindful breathing practice provided at the end of the Introduction. Use this time to just be here and now with each breath and the sensation of your breath as your belly rises and falls. You can also place your awareness on the sensation of your breath at your nostrils. This isn't a time for reflection; rather, use the felt sense of your breath as your way to be present.

If any thoughts or emotions arise for you, turn toward them for a moment with openness and curiosity. Notice if they affect your body in any way, and then redirect your attention back to your breath.

Be aware that this simple practice can be very helpful for easing anxiety. The next time you feel anxious, give it a try: As soon as you notice feelings of anxiety, notice where your breath is. If it's high in the chest, redirect it into the belly and see if you can allow it to settle in there and come and go on its own. After a few minutes, you may notice that the rhythm of your breath becomes more and more natural and at ease. Stay with the physical sensations of the breath in the belly as well as possible, and return to them when you wander. In a little while, check in on your mood state. You may discover, as many other people have, that feelings of anxiety begin to subside and diminish as you settle into this simple experience of being present with the breath moving in the belly.

Notes to Yourself

Again, please write for a few minutes in your journal on what you experienced during your mindful breathing.

a calling to remember

This chapter discussed the components of shyness to help you better understand how it creates so much suffering in your life. It's important to understand that fear and anxiety are natural and normal human experiences, and that efforts to avoid or escape these feelings just intensify them. A common problem in shyness and all anxiety disorders is the fear of fear itself. If you can learn to turn toward your fear with awareness and compassion, it may release its painful grip, allowing you to find new ways to respond to it.

I began this chapter with a phrase that was frequently repeated by my college friend David: "Life is fraught with peril!" David was particularly frightened of girls and often made this statement as he admired them from a distance and avoided them like the plague. I also admired girls and was scared of them, but I took the risk of extending myself to talk with them. David was wounded by his avoidance and loneliness, and I was wounded by many rejections and failures. Both of us suffered from our wounds, but I grew from mine and eventually grew out of much of my shyness. It was how I dealt with shyness that made a difference. I faced the perils of relationships and in the process learned to develop a new relationship with anxiety itself.

In this chapter, we looked at shyness patterns as habits of mind created and maintained as a way to keep safe. In this way, you're already starting to look at shyness from a more detached and aware perspective, which will help you better investigate your shyness pattern without identifying with it. In the chapters that follow, we'll take a closer look at the value of mindfulness in observing mental and emotional states and its role in healing. I'll provide practices, first to strengthen your mindful awareness, and then to help you work specifically on shyness and social anxiety. As your awareness grows, one of the things you may notice is that the part of you that's aware of anxiety is not itself anxious.

mindfulness and healing

We have what we seek. It is there all the time, and if we give it time it will make itself known to us.

—Thomas Merton

We all know what it is to find ourselves fully present in the here and now, if only for a few moments: Sitting on a bench at the park, you feel your own heart fill with happiness as you witness the joy of a young couple exalting in their baby's first steps. Or feeling a breeze, you look up to see hundreds of leaves release from the trees and suddenly have a sense of being at home and somehow gifted by what you've just witnessed. Sometimes by happy accident we find ourselves outside our self-enclosing habits and mental ruts, allowing us to come to our senses and show up to experience what is happening right here and right now. These moments often reveal something beautiful or even wondrous about the world, even if only in the dust that's swirling in a sunbeam. This generally involves a shift from thinking mode into the more experiential mode of the senses, which operates only in the present moment and may reveal many surprising things about what's happening right now. These are moments of awareness and, in a very real sense, liberation, but up until now you may have experienced them primarily as happy accidents.

Based on what you've read thus far, you now know that it's possible to promote these moments of awareness. Through mindfulness practice, you can consciously cultivate the quality of attention and presence that makes such moments of awareness possible. However, you may be thinking that it will take some work and dedication, and you're right about that. In case you wonder if it's worth your while, let's take a look at some of the benefits of mindfulness and how it can promote healing.

the value of awareness

Mindfulness is the awareness you experience when you are present for the moments of your life without judging them or trying to change them—and without judging or trying to change yourself. With practice, you can bring this kind of awareness to anything you're experiencing in your outer world, including relationships, or in your inner world of thoughts and emotions. You can even hold feelings like anxiety or fear in your awareness.

As discussed earlier, our lives are generally governed by patterns that we don't investigate even though they can be extremely predictable and create a great deal of suffering. Given that you frequently experience shyness, certain social cues probably throw you into an automatic mode in which you react in the same ways you've always reacted, time and time again. By turning your awareness inward, you can change your relationship to your thoughts and feelings. You'll find that you can observe and investigate shyness patterns, such as imagining the worst and avoidance, without getting caught up in them. Looking at habits of mind from this perspective, you can see how your thoughts are connected to your feelings and behaviors and recognize when you're succumbing to habits like self-doubt and avoidance, and this alone can help you not fall under the same old spell.

Awareness is an intrinsic element of your mind and body's self-healing system. It's always been a part of you, though perhaps you haven't exercised it much. If you haven't, you're certainly not alone. Awareness can only be exercised when you're in the present moment, and most of the time, most of us aren't. I once saw a bumper sticker that spoke to this all-too-human dilemma: "Having a good time. Wish I were here!" We're usually somewhere in an imaginary future or a worrisome past, or busily doing other things in our minds that override awareness of the here and now. But with some intention, we can come into that awareness and learn to observe our thoughts and emotions.

In Western culture, we've been socialized away from our immediate experience of the here and now and conditioned to try to perform what's expected of us. This conditioned performer is the aspect of self that creates much of the suffering in shyness. One of the most liberating discoveries you might make as you grow in mindfulness is that awareness is a greater part of you than the old habits of mind you're investigating. If that seems a bit abstract, read on. The research outlined below reveals some of the benefits of present-moment awareness.

mindfulness in medicine and psychotherapy

There is substantial evidence supporting the benefits of mindfulness for medical and psychological conditions (Orsillo and Roemer 2005). In addition to mindfulness-based stress reduction (MBSR), which has twenty-five years of supporting research and has been shown to be helpful with both psychological and medical conditions, three other mindfulness-based approaches have been developed solely for the treatment of psychological conditions such as anxiety, depression, and borderline personality disorder. These are mindfulness-based cognitive therapy (MBCT), acceptance and commitment therapy (ACT), and dialectical behavior therapy (DBT). (There is a good deal of research supporting these approaches as well, and you'll find resources for each of these psychotherapies at the back of this book.) For the purposes of this book, I'll provide a brief look at mindfulness-based stress reduction and mindfulness-based cognitive therapy and a bit of the supporting research.

Mindfulness-Based Stress Reduction

Dr. Jon Kabat-Zinn introduced the medical use of mindfulness in 1979, when he founded the Stress Reduction Clinic at the University of Massachusetts Medical Center. Known as mindfulness-based stress reduction, his program was the first application of mindfulness in a modern medical setting to help people with stress-related conditions like anxiety and chronic pain. This program, which involves the intensive cultivation of mindfulness skills, has repeatedly been shown to be helpful in reducing anxiety, depression, and the symptoms of many other stress-related illnesses. Dr. Kabat-Zinn and his colleagues have conducted research on the MBSR program since its inception and have accumulated an extraordinary body of data that documents the benefits of MBSR (Center for Mindfulness 2008).

Mindfulness-Based Cognitive Therapy

Mindfulness-based cognitive therapy (MBCT) has been demonstrated to be effective in helping with psychological conditions, especially depression (Segal, Williams, and Teasdale 2002; Williams et al. 2007). A central emphasis in MBCT is to modify attention rather than the contents of the mind, seeing thoughts and feelings as passing events rather than inherent aspects of self and recognizing that thoughts aren't always an accurate reflection of reality. MBCT emphasizes the cultivation of an awareness that is separate from and able to witness thoughts and uses this awareness as the agent of change in therapy. When we *decenter*, or shift our focus, from avoidant and control-oriented perspectives, we can see thoughts and feelings as transient events separate from ourselves (Segal, Williams, and Teasdale 2002).

Thoughts like "They don't like me" or "There's something wrong with me" can have a major impact on feelings of shyness and social anxiety. In fact, an enormous piece of the habitual pattern of shyness is taking such thoughts as accurate reflections of reality and repeatedly buying into them. Learning to observe these thoughts opens the door to a whole new way of relating to them. Thoughts are passing and insubstantial events, and their content is always changing.

scientific support for mindfulness

During nearly thirty years of practicing psychotherapy and thirty-five years of practicing meditation, I have witnessed a great many people make remarkable progress in reducing the suffering in their lives with meditation. Particularly in the MBSR program I've provided for the last twelve years, I've seen dramatic and significant reductions of anxiety and depression with mindfulness meditation. Similar observations have been documented in numerous research studies by Dr. Kabat-Zinn and his colleagues. In one of his earliest studies, in 1982, participants who completed an MBSR program showed a 50 percent reduction in psychological symptoms like anxiety and depression, as well as dramatic reductions in physical symptoms like pain (Kabat-Zinn 1982). Ten years later, another study showed that medical patients with generalized anxiety who completed an MBSR program experienced a 35 to 65 percent decrease in psychological symptoms such as anxiety and panic and a decreased frequency of panic attacks and medical symptoms (Kabat-Zinn et al. 1992). A three-year follow-up study found that these benefits were maintained or increased (Miller, Fletcher, and Kabat-Zinn 1995).

An ongoing study by Phillippe Goldin, Ph.D., at Stanford University is specifically aimed at measuring the effectiveness of MBSR in helping people with social anxiety. Using brain scans and numerous psychological measurement tools, Dr. Goldin is comparing the effectiveness of MBSR to both cognitive behavioral therapy and a wellness program. Final results of this research are expected to be published in 2012, but preliminary results indicate that both CBT and MBSR are effective interventions for shyness (Goldin 2008; 2009). These early research results indicate that MBSR significantly reduced social anxiety and significantly improved self-esteem and emotional regulation in the participants with social anxiety who completed the program. Specifically, Dr. Goldin's findings indicate that MBSR reduces negative evaluations, negative self-beliefs, and responses from the amygdala, a part of the brain considered to be the seat of fear, anger, and other powerful emotions. In addition, MBSR improves control and regulation of attention and cognitive regulation. Dr. Goldin suggests that one way MBSR improves emotional self-regulation (and reduces social anxiety) is by improving the ability to reinterpret the meaning of a situation to make it less disturbing.

In another interesting study, significant because it shows biological benefits of mindfulness meditation, twenty-five subjects were given a flu vaccine, then participated in an eight-week MBSR program. Over the eight-week period, brain activity and immune system biomarkers were measured and compared to a control group of sixteen people who were also given the flu vaccine but didn't participate in an MBSR program. The brain imaging results in this study showed that participants who meditated had significantly enhanced the electrical activity of the left frontal region of their brain, an area associated with self-calming and positive emotions. Results of immune function tests were also interesting, as they showed that these participants also had a significantly enhanced immune response to the flu vaccine as compared to the control group (Davidson et al. 2003).

If all of that discussion of research seems a bit technical, don't fret. What's important to know for your work with this book is that mindfulness-based and cognitive behavioral interventions have been shown to be effective for problematic shyness and social anxiety, and weaving these powerful tools together, which is the approach in this book, may well be the most effective way to address these interpersonal difficulties.

changing your brain mindfully

Until recently, it was believed that an adult brain couldn't generate enough new neurons to make much of a difference in its functioning. However, pioneering work by researchers such as Dr. Richard Davidson at the University of Wisconsin (2006) has demonstrated that the brain continues to grow and change throughout life. Dr. Davidson's research shows that not only are we always growing more neurons, but our emotions have a particularly powerful influence in this process and demonstrably modify our brains.

Using neuroimaging, Davidson has discovered that areas of the brain associated with positive emotions and good mood are considerably more active in people who have been practicing mindfulness meditation for a long time than they are in people who haven't. This indicates that there is more neural circuitry in these areas of the brain. Further, Davidson reports that even though some people are born with more "joy juice" than others—in other words, a greater capacity to experience pleasure—we are trainable. His research indicates that mindfulness can enhance our capacity for self-regulation and equanimity.

In fact, research indicates that we are self-creating and self-perpetuating in many ways, even to the extent that we can physically change our brains with our thoughts and emotions. Further, with attentional training, we can learn to alter and shape our brains to serve us in more positive ways (Davidson et al. 2003; Davidson 2006; Davidson 2009). New technological tools such as functional magnetic resonance imaging and positron-emission tomography have enabled scientists to document how the human brain forms neuropathways that it tends to follow again and again. These discoveries indicate that we have extraordinary influence on the development of our own brains, which are always changing in relation to how we use them. The mental and emotional states we attend to the most change our brains so we can experience more of those states. Indeed, it has been suggested that our minds are creating our brains to give expression to what our minds want or have become accustomed to (Siegel 2007c).

It's fascinating to see that science can now substantiate what has been known by the contemplative traditions for thousands of years: that the source of much of our pleasure and suffering is the mind. We create a great deal of our own happiness or suffering by our way of looking at things. Vietnamese mindfulness teacher Thich Nhat Hanh (2001) speaks to this dynamic, referring to incipient emotions as seeds. He teaches that we all have the seeds of difficult emotions within us and that the key is to not water those seeds. Rather, we must learn to nourish compassion, understanding, loving-kindness, and other positive qualities.

more than a technique

Although mindfulness is being brought into many contexts for health and healing, be aware that mindfulness is much more than a new treatment technique to be employed in efforts of fix or improve ourselves. Throughout his numerous books and thousands of presentations, Dr. Jon Kabat-Zinn emphasizes again and again that mindfulness is a state of being and a way of life, not simply an instrument in the doctor's proverbial black bag. As a way of life, mindfulness has no goal. In fact, two of the key elements of mindfulness are nonjudging and nonstriving. The moment you direct your attention to a goal you want to accomplish, you've left the mindfulness mode.

This isn't to say that goals and plans to realize them aren't useful, and of course they don't disappear as we grow in mindfulness. Mental faculties that review the past, anticipate the future, and conceive of and work toward goals are absolutely essential. Mindfulness isn't antithetical or opposed to this; rather, it enables us to use these faculties more deliberately and recognize them as discrete elements of our consciousness, not the whole of who we are. Sometimes we succeed in a goal, and sometimes we fail. Through mindfulness, we may learn to be less attached and reactive in regard to both our failures and our successes.

And despite its growing popularity in the Western world, the practice of mindfulness certainly isn't new. It's been practiced within most of the world's spiritual and religious traditions for thousands of years as a way to awaken to truth and free ourselves from suffering. The practices and elements of mindfulness within the 2,600-year-old Buddhist tradition lend themselves particularly well to applications in medicine and psychotherapy, but it's important to acknowledge that mindfulness is too expansive and universal to be encompassed by any single tradition, be it spiritual, medical, or philosophical. The compassionate awareness of mindfulness is intrinsic to all human beings, and we can all nurture and cultivate this awareness, no matter what the context of our lives or our orientation in the world.

a mindful view of shyness

Essentially, a mindful view of anything means being as present as possible in your moment-to-moment experience and noticing whatever you notice without judging or striving. By practicing mindfulness, you can gradually grow more skillful at noticing your way of looking at and doing things. When you make shyness the object of your awareness, you'll soon notice that you can't really find a thing called shyness to investigate. What you will find is particular thoughts, emotions, sensations, and behaviors that compose your experience of shyness. Paying attention to the interplay of these four dimensions of shyness will reveal the ways in which your body and mind are connected. It will also allow you to recognize how certain thoughts are connected to certain emotions, which are in turn connected to certain physical sensations and to an urge to do something. For example, in the times of my life when I was most shy, in many social situations I thought that people didn't like me (a thought), and then I felt anxious (an emotion). As I glanced around, sometimes it really seemed that people were looking at me funny (a projection). I would notice my heart beating faster and my throat feeling tight (physical sensations) and often decided to go somewhere else (a behavior) to do something else that suddenly seemed much more appealing (escape and isolation).

When you bring mindful awareness into a sequence like this, it becomes much more evident that not all thoughts are true, and that some of your emotions and behaviors are simply deeply ingrained habits. Fortunately, you can take the whole thing off of automatic pilot if you want.

A Multiplicity of Selves

Looking into your thoughts, emotions, sensations, and behaviors helps you see that there are many ways to be you, but it is also likely to reveal that you tend to remain confined in some rather narrowly defined self-concepts. You may have already discovered that it can be extremely difficult to deliberately change your self-concept. In fact, it takes something more powerful than an intention to change; you need to have a personal experience that there is more to you than you thought.

Your way of looking at and thinking about yourself is essentially a collection of memories and ideas, of which your story is comprised: "I'm a sensitive person." "I'm a victim." "I'm a survivor." Is this who you really are? In telling and retelling your story to yourself, you maintain that identity and lose track of your wholeness, the living inner core that is more who you are than the stories you tell yourself or anyone else. What we generally don't notice is that the stories we tell ourselves about ourselves are often yet more habits of mind with which we've come to identify. However, they're just stories, and through mindfulness we can discover deeper aspects of who we are, change our way of looking at ourselves, and open the door to wider possibilities for our lives. Feeling shy, for example, may become just a quality of personality that is part of your wholeness but no longer defines and restricts your life.

A mindful view of shyness is therefore quite different from a more typical stance, which would seek to reduce, control, or somehow escape shyness. Mindfulness is being with things as they are and being open to discovery.

The Shyness Identity

From the perspective of mindfulness, you can see that problematic shyness or the sense of a self you identify as shy isn't a static thing. Its components of self-judgments, painful emotions, and avoidance behaviors are always evolving in relation to each other. It actually takes a lot of work to maintain the painfully shy identity as you try to be invisible, not draw attention to yourself, slip away without being noticed, or otherwise perpetuate the illusion of being disconnected from others. Suppose you were to stop working so hard at shoring up these defenses between you and everyone else? What else could you do with all of that energy? As mindful awareness exposes that part of you that works to maintain a familiar personal narrative, just witnessing how you construct and repeat the story can help you disidentify with it.

• Discoveries on the Path: *Marilyn's Story*

Though Marilyn had completed a mindfulness-based stress reduction program and had been meditating every day for months, she still suffered from anxiety, so she called me to see if we might help her find some relief through therapy. In her meditation practice, she was plagued by the same relentless and cruel internal critic that had haunted her all her life and insinuated itself into nearly everything she did. She even blamed herself for blaming herself: "Why can't I do or say anything without blaming myself for doing it wrong? Why can't I just be like everyone else? Why can't I even meditate without criticizing myself?" She knew that this ugly habit of self-blaming and self-shaming essentially echoed the cruel words and hateful attacks she had heard from her mother before she finally ran away from home at age fifteen. "I hated her words when I was a kid. Why do I have to listen to them for the rest of my life?"

Though she was clearly well aware that this had caused her suffering for many years, Marilyn couldn't let go of the self-blaming and self-shaming and felt profoundly unworthy. Our work together began with shifting her intention from trying to get rid of this critic to getting to know it better and understanding it.

After we had worked together for a while, Marilyn developed some skill in regulating her emotions as she investigated the comments of this internal critic. From this newfound sense of acceptance and equanimity, she decided to go to an extended meditation retreat to see if she might become even more skillful in not falling for the critic's nasty judgments. After a week at the retreat, she made an important discovery. While sitting in a rare and spacious state of mind where, for once, she wasn't under attack from the critic, she discovered that another part of her was actively searching for something that was wrong with her. She was astonished to realize that the critic wasn't some disembodied voice from her mother—it was her! She was scanning to find something wrong with the way she was meditating, had assisted with serving lunch, had spoken to the teacher in an interview… She was actually trying to create new stories to make herself feel flawed.

As she leaned into this feeling, an enormous sense of grief swept through her—and also a powerful understanding: all of this self-blaming was a way to keep her distracted from the anguish of never being loved. Her internal storyteller was creating her anxiety as a means to avoid deeper pain. As she turned toward her deeper and more legitimate anguish with loving-kindness and compassion, she felt something soften in her body and open to the longing within her that she had overlooked and pushed aside time and time again. She saw that beyond and within her shyness identity, which never wanted to be seen or even exist, was a part of herself that actually yearned to be seen and to be loved.

Although it may seem counterintuitive, you may need to spend quality time with something as obnoxious as an internal critic in order to appease it. Like Marilyn, you may find that these parts of yourself are trying to help you in their own misguided way. Exploring them may help you find deeper dimensions of yourself that call for your love and self-compassion. In fact, you're likely to find that the critic itself needs your love (Stone and Stone 1998). Little by little, through mindful awareness you can learn to bring the light of compassion to even the darkest parts of yourself. As you do, things have a way of lightening up!

One important note on Marilyn's story: When she decided to go on the extended meditation retreat, I agreed to be available to her by phone if something overwhelming came up and she needed support. While meditation can provide great insight, it can sometimes open the door to thoughts, emotions, and sensations that may initially feel overwhelming, particularly if you've shut them out for a long time. Meditation isn't a substitute for therapy, particularly when you are working with a life trauma. If your practice brings up material that feels overwhelming, it's a good idea to obtain support from a trusted friend, teacher, or therapist.

Many of your concepts of self will change if they're no longer supported by an inflexible personal narrative. By attending to your thoughts as they arise, you'll see that you are not your thoughts. As you watch them come and go, you'll see that they are simply passing experiences, as are the emotions and sensations attached to them. As such, you can allow them to arise and pass without buying into them or identifying with them. Your thoughts and emotions are not you, they're just what you happen to be thinking or feeling at that moment. The wide-open awareness that witnesses these constantly changing mental events is already whole and at peace. You don't have to create this state of awareness; it's already a part of your consciousness, even though it may be somewhat neglected at this point. The mindfulness practices you'll learn throughout this book will help you cultivate this awareness so that you might operate from it as a way of life. If this feels a bit esoteric at this point, don't worry; we'll explore it at length in chapter 5.

a nonrational mental faculty

Most people attempt to overcome shyness using rational thought, which isn't surprising, as this is the mental orientation in which we generally spend most of our time. In this mind-set, we employ discursive reasoning, words, and concepts to analyze problems and pursue answers. Most of us run our lives almost entirely with this kind of thinking, and it's enormously valuable in some regards, like giving us the ability to establish goals and then employ logic and analysis to achieve those goals. This is the kind of thinking that enables us to create lifesaving medications or build spacecraft, and it sometimes comes in handy for figuring out where you misplaced your car keys, but it can cause problems when it's the only approach you use to manage fear or social anxiety.

One of the problems with this approach is that it's linear and goal oriented, whereas feelings are neither. You may have already discovered that you can't get rid of anxious thoughts and feelings just because they're troublemakers and you don't want them. In fact, the more you try to eradicate them, the more entrenched and repetitive they become.

In contrast to a rational approach to shyness, which tends to analyze, judge, and use the harsher taskmaster of the will, the principle work of a mindfulness-based approach is cultivating faculties such as awareness, intuition, acceptance, and compassion via an approach that is nonjudging and nonstriving. There's much to be discovered along the mindful path. Awareness and openness have revealed some of the greatest discoveries of science though happenstance, such as Friedrich Kekulé discovering the structure of the benzene ring in a day dream, or Alexander Fleming's chance discovery of penicillin due to contamination of a petri dish. These discoveries weren't made by unerring application of the scientific method, but by paying attention to a wider reality.

Similarly, mindfulness-based approaches to stress and anxiety are beneficial not because they facilitate great accomplishments, but because they enable great discoveries. Louis Pasteur maintained that chance favors the prepared mind, and I certainly agree—with the proviso that sometimes the best preparation is to settle down, come into mindful awareness, and be open to whatever comes up. Consider the times when you finally found your car keys or glasses after you calmed down and quit frantically searching for them. When you let go of a goal orientation, you may discover things that reason and striving can't figure out. When you return to your senses and are present, you're no longer being governed by an internal dialogue that distracts you, and in the case of shyness, tends to isolate you from everyone around you. When you aren't attending to whatever anxiety-provoking self-talk may be going on in your head, you'll be free to see and respond to what this moment calls for.

You can spend years and enormous resources trying to get rid of anxiety. Yet all the while you might find the freedom you want by regarding it from a different point of view—one that's more curious and accepting than it is critical and rejecting. This type of checking in to discover who you are and where you are is the essence of both informal and formal meditation practice. Remember, you can't plot a course to a particular destination if you don't know where you are in the first place. That said, don't worry too much about getting lost. No matter how hard you try to pay attention along the way, you're bound to get lost from time to time. It's not the end of the world. All you need to do is stop, tune in to your awareness, and bring your attention back to the now. In meditation circles, this is referred to as beginning again, and it will be a frequent activity along your path of mindfulness, as it is for everyone. In fact, beginning again is the principle way you progress.

Getting lost gives you the chance to consult your mindful compass and feel your emotions and sensations. Are they pleasant, unpleasant, or neutral? Is your primary heading self-compassion? Consulting this compass is how you stay found. Every time you consult it, you return to awareness of the present moment, rather than ruminations about the past or projections of the future. This will free you from automatic habits of mind and allow you to be responsive rather than reactive to the environment and situations in which you find yourself.

to be or to do—that is the question

We human beings have two principle modes of operation: being mode and doing mode (Williams et al. 2007). Being mode offers resources for learning, healing, and well-being that doing mode can't access. In being mode there is no judgment or striving, whereas in doing mode it's hard to stop judging and striving.

When we operate from mindful awareness, we're in being mode. When we operate from the goal-oriented mind, we're in doing mode— the mind state that creates and perpetuates shyness patterns and, as you may have noticed, hasn't been able to break free of those patterns. To paraphrase Albert Einstein, we can't solve our problems using the same level of thinking that created them. In other words, we need to think outside the box.

When you aren't so intent on doing something about shyness, you can access the mode in which you are simply being with shyness, or letting shyness be. This allows you to look into your shyness pattern, which you may discover is mostly created by your doing mode of operation. Just by shifting to being mode, you can find some distance from those patterns of thought and emotion and stop believing all the critical things you tell yourself about yourself or the scary things you imagine as you get caught up in thinking about the future.

Many years ago, I had just turned in the final thesis for my master's degree in psychology and religion. As I was leaving the university campus and my official status as a student, I stopped in the student union to use the restroom. Although I had spent years trying to bridge the worlds of science and religion, I still hadn't found a way to reconcile their differences. Amazingly, I found the solution that afternoon—on the bathroom wall, of all places. Someone had written, "To be is to do—Descartes." Someone else had written, "To be, don't do—Lao Tsu." Lastly, someone else had written, "Do, be, do, be, do—Frank Sinatra." That was the answer: First immerse yourself in being, then express it, then immerse yourself again, then express it, then immerse yourself again.

The problem with many of our efforts to change and be happy is that they're essentially driven by a part of ourselves that really doesn't know how to free us from suffering or make us happy. When we are pursuing what we want or trying to avoid what we fear, we rarely notice what we have right here and now. If we can let go of chasing after what we think we need and settle into what we already have, we can discover a quality of being that is already whole and free from suffering, just as it is. And if we can stop trying to be someone we aren't, we might just discover who we really are.

mindfulness practice:
Mindful Breathing

In the rest of this book, we'll explore a variety of mindfulness techniques, many focused on helping you with problematic shyness. But for now, it's useful for you to simply continue to practice mindfulness of your breath, as this is a touchstone you can always come back to. Continued practice of mindful breathing will create a solid foundation of mindfulness that you can build on as you work forward in this book.

Please pause for five or ten minutes, or as long as you like, to practice mindful breathing as described in the introduction. Remember the intention to simply be present with the sensation of your breath coming and going. When thoughts and emotions come up, as they inevitably will, just gently redirect your attention back to your breath—the rise and fall of your belly or the sensation of your breath at your nostrils.

You may notice many things about how your breath interacts with different mental and emotional states, such as anxiety, when you are practicing. The invitation with these discoveries is to make silent note of them, let them be, and return your attention to the felt sense of the breath in the belly. The central intention is to just be present with these sensations.

Notes to Yourself

Again, take a few minutes to write in your journal about what you experienced during your mindful breathing. After you finish writing, set your journal down, once again close your eyes, and spend a couple more minutes with the rising and falling movement of your belly as you breathe.

a calling to remember

This chapter explored some of the benefits of mindfulness and, more specifically, how it can help you see your shyness identity and understand how it's constructed and maintained. Know that just by looking into your shyness pattern in a nonjudgmental way, you are employing your faculty of awareness, and that alone will enable you to become a little more free from that pattern. Remember that when you're centered in awareness, you aren't centered in thoughts and are no longer subject to the tyranny of mental and behavioral habits that create and perpetuate shyness and social anxiety.

It's important to use your mindful compass. This simple but powerful orientation tool can help you recenter yourself in awareness during stressful moments. As you turn toward your thoughts, emotions, sensations, and behaviors with awareness, you can notice if they are pleasant, unpleasant, or neutral and how they're interconnected. As you come to your senses, being here and now in each new breath, you can respond rather than react to what's before you.

In part 2, we'll explore the basics of mindfulness through a wider variety of practices. We'll also look at ways of embracing the nonverbal world. This is a powerful means of loosening the grip of the rational, discursive mind and its doing mode.

PART II

coming home to yourself

The time will come
When with elation,
you will greet yourself arriving
at your own door in your own mirror,
and each will smile at the other's welcome,

and say, sit here. Eat.
You will love again the stranger who was your self.
Give wine. Give bread. Give back your heart
to itself, to the stranger who has loved you

all your life, whom you have ignored
for another, who knows you by heart.
Take down the love letters from the bookshelf,

the photographs, the desperate notes,
peel your own image from the mirror.
Sit. Feast on your life.

—Derek Walcott, "Love after Love"

practicing 3 mindfulness

I never came upon any of my discoveries through the process of rational thinking.

—Albert Einstein

There is no more important or valuable gift you might receive from your work with this book than the practice of mindfulness meditation. Nothing else you learn here will do more to help you with shyness and social anxiety. The interesting thing about this gift is that you are the only one who can give it to yourself. Mindfulness meditation isn't complicated. It happens every time you bring your attention to the present moment without judging or trying to change what you're experiencing, and the more you practice it, the more it flourishes. It can become as familiar and intimate to you as the sensation of your breath, and you can experience it anytime, anyplace—at home eating dinner, sitting in a traffic jam on the freeway, while walking around the block.

compassionate presence

A common mistake of many people who feel shy is believing that the energy we need to get by and finally be okay is somewhere "out there" in the form of acceptance, approval, appreciation, or support and that not getting it leads to suffering. People have a variety of beliefs about the reasons why they can't get it, like "I'm too skittish (or needy or fat or skinny—you name it)." What we don't realize is that the principle energy we need is actually inside us and has been all along, in the form of self-compassion. It's like we have a deep well within us that has all the water we could ever need, but we don't realize it's there. We go about with a little cup that's half full, hoping to get a few more drops and afraid that someone might knock what little we have out of our hands.

Meditation practice is a way to nourish and grow kindness and self-compassion. Sitting quietly, you notice that your mind has eloped with you into some imaginary scene in the future. You then notice a feeling of frustration with your wayward mind. That moment of frustration is a perfect place to practice mercy and kindness. Since this is something that minds tend to do quite a lot, these sorts of meditation mini dramas offer many opportunities to practice self-compassion. Having your mind wander off isn't really such a terrible thing; it's just what minds do. Attending to these wanderings with kindness and self-compassion is a very real and powerful way to create happiness and peace in your life rather than anxiety and fear. When you notice that your mind is somewhere other than where you intended, smile to yourself and gently feel into that place for a moment or two to see where you've gone. Is it the future, the past, or some worry or judgment? Then kindly acknowledge what you find there, let it be, and return your attention to your object of intention. Begin again.

At a meditation retreat many years ago, mindfulness teacher Jack Kornfield spoke of this as "puppy training." As you try to train your puppy to stay, you quickly discover that the puppy has very different ideas of what it's going to do and only has an attention span of a few nanoseconds before it darts off and does something you really don't want, like piddle on the carpet. He cautioned against beating up the puppy and advised being kind instead. Begin again. Stay.

Noticing where your mind wanders during meditation practice will provide opportunities to extend kindness and compassion to yourself in other ways, beyond just accepting the wandering of your mind. Like most of us, your mind probably sometimes goes to places where you feel frightened, unhappy, hurt, or disturbed. As you feel into these places, notice if your heart is calling out for some particular expression of loving-kindness and know that mindful awareness can enable you to respond to it.

What is your heart calling out for? By listening to it rather than trying to make it be quiet, you may learn how to respond to it with self-compassion. First listen to find where the hurt is under the anger, anxiety, or critical reaction that's come up. Try to feel deeply into your heart and ask yourself, "What is the pain that's underneath this reaction?" Something will rise to greet you and say things like "I've been wronged," "This bad thing happened to me," "I've been hurt," "I've done something wrong," or "I've done something bad."

Whatever you find, open your heart to feel it deeply with the spirit of self-compassion, and extend a few kind or supportive words to this place in yourself. Here are some words of loving-kindness and self-compassion you might say to yourself at these times. See if any of them resonate with you:

- I care for this hurt and frightened heart.
- I care for this suffering.
- These feelings matter.
- Even if all others fail me, I will be there for myself.
- I will take care of myself.
- I will honor myself.
- I will not abandon myself.
- Even if I fail myself or have failed myself, I will forgive myself.
- I can begin again.

Every time you turn to these places of hurt and longing with loving-kindness, you actively create compassionate presence, and this can become the very foundation of your meditation practice.

the well

Years ago I spent a lot of money to have a well drilled on my land. I watched with anticipation as the contractor turned on the spigot at the well for the first time. Brownish, thick water dripped slowly onto the ground. My thoughts were disturbing, to say the least. "Be patient," the contractor told me. "Each drop of water is carrying out a little more sediment with it. It may take some time, but soon you'll see more water." Sure enough, in a few hours the water was clearer and dripping more rapidly, and by nightfall there was a steady stream of clear water.

Because you have felt shy for so long, treating yourself with compassion and loving-kindness may be foreign to you and probably exactly the opposite of how you've treated yourself for many years. So if you turn on the tap of your new well of self-compassion and it's only dripping out thick, brownish little globs, that's okay. Leave the tap open and return to it again and again. In time, more of the channel will open, and compassion will flow more freely and abundantly.

do you know where your mind is?

As you grow in mindful awareness, you'll gradually find that you can choose whether or not to enter into and perpetuate self-defeating patterns of thought and behavior. Although we tend to identify with these self-defeating patterns, they have no real substance and are therefore sometimes called the "conditioned self" or the "false self." The conditioned self is a clamor of wanting and aversion, judging and striving, pursuing and escaping that creates a state of general malaise and discontent.

There's enormous value in recognizing and identifying the agitated and dissatisfied part of your mind. One extraordinary benefit is the discovery that the part of you that is aware of these mental activities is not itself agitated or dissatisfied and that you can witness the chattering in your head and not identify with it. This shift in perspective brings the question "Who is this compassionate witness of my thoughts and emotions?" This self-inquiry can help you discover a deeper sense of being and wholeness. You can't access this gift of mindfulness meditation if you're judging and striving or trying to get somewhere other than where you are. It arrives when you come home to yourself and, in the words of the poet Derek Walcott, "give back your heart to itself, to the stranger that has loved you all your life" (1976, p. 74). It's only when you stop your pursuit of something more or better can you come home to the wholeness that has been the inner core of your being all along.

Being mindfully aware of where you are calls forth a certain acceptance of yourself as you are for now. It reveals the truth. Though it may not be the truth you prefer, it is the truth, and as such is the starting point for working with those things that create suffering in your life. Accepting things as they are frees you from the never-ending cycle of self-improvement or self-protection that results from self-judgment and striving. The practice of mindfulness reveals your essential, unconditioned nature precisely because you are no longer trying to be different.

see for yourself exercise 1:
Eating a Raisin

Here's a simple exercise that will provide you with a taste of mindfulness. Find a raisin or some other small food object that you can practice this exercise with. It won't take a great deal of time, and it will provide insight that will help you with the mindfulness practices ahead. Find a spot where you can sit comfortably without any distractions such as the TV or music, and where you can have some time and space to yourself to practice a little mindful eating.

Hold the raisin in your hand and bring as much curiosity to it as you can. It may help to pretend that you've never seen one of these objects before and that you're hungry and want to determine if this is something that you can eat. You'll want to examine it closely.

1. **Looking:** Because vision is often such a dominant sensation, please turn to that sense first and take in all that you can see from looking at this object. Take in its colors, dimensions, shapes, and contours. Do this as if you were a scientist and need to describe what you see in purely descriptive, objective terms. At the same time, notice that there's a difference between directly seeing this object in your hand and the words you use to describe it. Next, read the instructions below, then close your eyes as you try the rest of these sensations.

2. **Touching:** Take in all that you can feel of this object with your fingers: textures and qualities like softness, hardness,

resiliency, smoothness, or stickiness. It has a certain cool-ness or warmth and maybe even a weight that is evident.

3. **Smelling:** When you're ready, bring this object to your nos-trils and breathe in whatever scent you can detect. Is it sweet or pungent or spicy? Does it have any odor at all?

4. **Listening:** As silly as it sounds (and to the surprise of many a doubting Thomas who has tried this exercise), you might be able to hear something in this object if you manipulate it with your fingers by your ear.

5. **Bringing it to your lips:** I've been watching my six-month-old grandson with a great deal of interest lately (as all smitten grandparents do) and have noticed that it's no small thing to discover that you can bring things to your lips. Notice how your arms, hands, and fingers move in order to place this object in your mouth. Notice what happens in your mouth as you do so.

6. **Tasting:** Before you begin to chew this object, move it around in your mouth a little to explore it a bit more. Notice if its size, temperature, or softness has changed. Gently chew it without breaking the skin just yet, and notice if you can sense its moistness or dryness. When you like, go ahead and bite into this object. Does this release any flavors? Can you sense those flavors from different places on your tongue? Notice how your tongue can so expertly guide what you're chewing to different areas of your teeth without getting bit itself. Notice what's inside of the object as you chew it.

7. **Swallowing:** At some point you'll feel an urge to swallow this object. See if you can spend a moment with that urge; this will bring a certain amount of attention to your inten-tion. Finally, when you do swallow this object, notice what remains in your mouth. Take in any lingering sensations such as aftertaste or feelings in your throat as this now very changed object moves down into your body.

You may be surprised how much you can experience with a single raisin. It's also a simple way to become aware of how much you can miss when you aren't present or really attending to what you're eating—or anything else for that matter. Though I've done this exercise many times with thousands of people, I still hear new discoveries about raisins that I've never heard or thought of before.

If this is possible for such a simple experience as eating a raisin, how much richness is there in your life that you might experience if you were to show up for the present moment with this kind of wide-open awareness? What might you discover about yourself, your talents, and your potential that you haven't noticed before?

Notes to Yourself

Take some time to write in your journal about what you experienced during the raisin exercise. You may want to go back over the steps outlined above to record what you sensed in each, and then make a few notes about your overall experience.

attitudes of mindfulness

Mindfulness is built on the foundation of certain attitudes: beginner's mind, nonjudging, nonstriving, acknowledgment and acceptance, and letting be and letting go. Let's take a closer look at each of these attitudes, as all of them are helpful in their own right, in addition to supporting mindfulness practice. As you'll see, these attitudes are complementary, and in some cases they overlap or share certain qualities.

Beginner's Mind

Beginner's mind means being present and looking at what you experience with a fresh perspective, like a child who is experiencing something for the first time. With beginner's mind there is much room for discovery, not only of what's new or as yet unexperienced, but also of the newness in familiar things and situations. With beginner's eyes, you see that *everything* is new, and that nothing has ever been experienced just like this before. There's never been another sunset exactly like this one, or another mango, or even another moment. From this point of view, it's all new and we're always beginning again. What an incredible opportunity!

In your mindfulness practice, beginner's mind will help you begin again each time you find that you've drifted into some other mental activity, whether rehashing a disagreement with a coworker, thinking about what's for dinner, or judging your meditation practice. Every time you find your mind in an imaginary future, a memory of the past, or some other place, you can gently remind yourself to come back to the here and now.

Nonjudging

We all have seemingly endless opportunities to practice nonjudging, because all human beings do quite a bit of judging. Even creating the intention to be nonjudging can create yet another thing to judge yourself about, as you can now judge yourself when you catch yourself judging! To develop a nonjudgmental attitude in your practice, don't assign values to your mental, emotional, or sensory experiences. Rather than viewing them as good or bad, or right or wrong, simply acknowledge what you experience for what it is.

Nonstriving

Nonstriving means being with things as they are without trying to change anything, including yourself. When you bring the intention of nonstriving into your moment-to-moment life, you no longer try to get to another time or place or condition, and likewise no longer try to get away from anything or anyplace. To practice nonstriving is to drop all end-gaining.

Because this concept is so foreign to our culture, it may be helpful to look at some of the ways that striving can actually interfere with attaining a goal. I'm sure you've had the experience of searching for something only to find you had it all along. Maybe you darted about looking for your sunglasses, only to find them on your own head. Or maybe you couldn't find the cheese in your own refrigerator until a friend pointed out that it was sitting prominently on the shelf right in front of you. When you're in striving mode, you can become so intent on the effort to attain the object of your desire that you overlook what's right in front of you. This particular difficulty of the seeker is portrayed in the parable about the pearl diver who failed to notice a giant pearl sitting next to an oyster because he wasn't looking for pearls, he was looking for oysters!

This is why nonstriving is such a key aspect of mindfulness meditation. Bringing this intention to your practice is anything but passive; it requires a deliberate shift from trying and achieving to allowing and discovering. It may seem that this doesn't facilitate change, but paradoxically, by practicing nonstriving you really do move forward. It's just a more gentle and patient way to progress.

Acknowledgement and Acceptance

Acknowledgment means validating what you experience. It's just calling a spade a spade without labeling it as wanted or unwanted, good or bad. Acceptance means having the intention to receive unconditionally whatever you've acknowledged as your experience. While acceptance means receiving the truth of your experience, it doesn't imply passive submission to external events or circumstances that may be harmful to you. If accepting the truth of your experience reveals that something is harmful to you or someone is abusive or truly menacing, it's probably appropriate to do everything in your power to change the situation. When working with inner experiences, such as a painful memory, sometimes the most skillful response is to acknowledge the truth of that experience with an intention that someday your acknowledgment could grow into acceptance.

Letting Be and Letting Go

Letting be is the intention to meet your internal experience without trying to either push it away or cling to it. This is a way to sit with things as they are and leave them as they are, without exerting any effort to do anything with them. It's been said that letting go is a powerful way to free yourself from suffering. While there is profound truth in this, letting go isn't always a simple choice. As with acceptance, it can seem to imply passive submission or acquiescence to things that are abhorrent. That isn't my intention. In mindfulness practice, "letting go" refers to how you relate to your own impulses to cling to or push away your experiences. Mindfulness involves letting go of those impulses again and again and developing an attitude of nonattachment in which you let go of your desire for things to be different than they are.

Using These Attitudes to Build Your Practice

Each of the attitudes we've just reviewed can be a powerful ally in working with your mind when it wanders during meditation practice. When you notice that your mind has wandered away from this moment, you might pause for a moment and feel into the place where it's wandered. Acknowledge it in some way, such as with the word "worrying," "planning," or whatever seems to best describe the mental activity your mind has been pursuing. Then, letting it be, begin again. There are, of course, many opportunities in this process to practice nonjudgment and extend self-compassion. These are approaches you'll use again and again during your meditation practice. In fact, these are the ways you build your practice and grow in mindfulness.

concentration practice and nonconcentration practice

There are essentially two forms of meditation practice. *Concentration* practice is directing your attention to something specific, such as your breath, an image, or a sound, and sustaining that attention until your mind becomes at one with the object of your focus. The raisin exercise and mindfulness of the breath are concentration practices, as are the body scan and "narrow-gauge" walking practices you'll learn in chapter 4. Loving-kindness meditation, which I'll discuss at length later in the book, is also a form of concentration practice. Within this unwavering attention, you will experience various levels of absorption and tranquility, and finer and finer degrees of stillness. This is like a spotlight that narrows its focus to carefully illuminate one object and then follows that object like a spotlight might follow an actor on stage.

Nonconcentration practice is expanding your attention to notice the beginnings and endings of breath, sensations, or mental phenomena, allowing you to begin to directly experience their impermanent nature. It's more like a floodlight that illuminates the whole stage. True mindfulness is a nonconcentration meditation practice and can be seen as pure awareness that's receptive to everything in the internal and external environment. As such, it can employ any experience—thoughts, emotions, or sensory stimuli—as a way to show up and be present. In chapter 7, you'll have an opportunity to explore nonconcentration meditation with the practice of choiceless awareness. As you'll see, you can build and grow into this spacious kind of awareness by training with concentration practices like conscious breathing.

mindfulness practice:
Mindfulness of the Body

In the following practice, you'll gradually expand your mindful breathing to become mindful of the body as a whole. As you take time to be fully present with your breath, you'll eventually discover that you feel it not only in your belly, chest, and nostrils, but also in subtle and not so subtle ways all over your body. Breathing in, you feel your lower back and the sides of your body expand a little. Notice that there's a sound to the breath and a consistent rhythm that sometimes changes a little just because you're paying attention to it. When you are really present for it, you'll find that your breath is a marvel and a miraculous expression of life itself. Is it any wonder that mindfulness of breathing and the body is a time-honored practice that has provided a path of meditation for untold numbers of people for thousands of years?

Part of the beauty and power of this practice lies in its simplicity and convenience; your breath is always right here, right now, offering you a way to be present in your body for this moment in your life. Each moment of this simple presence that you give yourself is a moment of mindfulness. Remember, all of life is really lived in the present moment. This is your chance to learn to be fully present within it.

To do this practice, choose a place that's as quiet as possible and where you won't be bothered by people, television, telephones, music, and so on. Consider this as a time you give to yourself as a gift. This is your time to just be. Before you begin the practice, read through the instructions several times until you're familiar with them so that you can proceed without consulting the book, or if you prefer, record these instructions for yourself and replay them for your practice. If you do choose to record the instructions, be sure to observe the pauses I've included periodically.

Do this practice in a seated position, either on a chair or on a cushion that supports your body in a way that allows you to sit upright, with some alignment in your head, neck, and body and a sense of dignity in your posture. As you take your place, please close your eyes and extend appreciation to yourself for taking this time to care for yourself. Know that you are giving yourself a gift of kindness.

Your posture should be neither too tight nor too loose, just comfortable and right for you, like a well-tuned string on a musical instrument. Rest your feet and legs in a way that they are fully supported and comfortable. If you're sitting on the floor, find a way to sit that feels stable, perhaps cross-legged with your knees resting on the floor if this is comfortable for you. You can use pillows to make this posture as comfortable as possible. Find a place to rest your hands where they're comfortable and at ease. Notice the places in your body where you're being supported, ultimately by the earth beneath you via the floor and cushion or chair. Settle into these places. Close your eyes or, if you prefer, leave them slightly open, with your gaze soft and directed somewhere on the floor a little ahead of you.

1. Bring your attention to your belly and notice it moving with your breath. Use the sensations of the belly rising and falling as your way to be present. (Pause for two minutes.)

2. Breathing normally and naturally, let your breath come and go as it will, without trying to change it in any way. As you settle into awareness of your breath, the spaces between breaths may become more evident, and you may notice that the pace and quality of your breath seems to change from time to time. Just acknowledge these slight variations and let them be.

3. You may also notice other observations and thoughts about your breath, or many other topics that the thinking mind will come up with. Notice this and label it as "wandering" or "thinking," then simply return to the physical sensation of the breath. Do this every time your mind wanders.

4. Be present. Your body knows how to breathe you, and you can be present for the full duration of each in breath and each out breath. Let this felt sense of the breath now guide you into feeling your body as a whole, sitting and noticing whatever sensation is most prominent to you. At one moment you notice an itch on your cheek, at another, the need to swallow. Notice that sensations are constantly changing and that you don't need to interpret them, judge them, or really do anything at all other than be aware of them. Be present for bodily sensations as they come up and recede just as ocean waves come up and recede. Notice that just as no two waves are alike, no two moments are alike. (Pause for five minutes.)

5. Allow your attention to settle in to the most prominent sensation for as long as you like as a way to anchor yourself in the present moment. At one moment your body may feel too cool, at another too warm. An ache in your knee or your buttocks is an opportunity to be present and may change in some way as you bring the fullness of your attention to it. Sensations may be more or less intense in any given moment, or you may experience a combination of sensations. Discomfort may call you to mindfully rearrange your body in some way. This is perfectly alright and can be done with a spirit of self-compassion. If you do move, notice the intention to move and then the sensations of transitioning into movement, then movement itself, then the return to stillness. Notice how each sensation gives you a way to ground yourself in the experience of now. Alert, at ease. Being present.

6. Please stay with this practice for twenty to thirty minutes, or longer if you like, and when you stop, thank yourself for taking the time to practice mindfulness.

Notes to Yourself

Take some time to write about your practice in your journal. You may find some value in acknowledging the mental, emotional, and physical experiences you noticed as you did this practice and what, if anything, you resisted being with or feeling in your body.

mindful inquiry

As you practice mindfulness of the body, you'll notice that sometimes you can be aware of thoughts and emotions coming and going and let them be while you stay present with the breath. You'll also find that you lose track of your body and the current moment many times as you become involved in thoughts or emotions. You can become more aware of the nature and function of these distractions by spending a few moments with them to see what you can discover there. This is mindful inquiry.

Often, mental events that capture your attention and draw you into them have come around in your consciousness many, many times before. These kinds of thoughts and feelings, particularly those that fuel your shyness patterns, can yield important insights if you bring the light of awareness to them during your meditation practice. This gives you a chance to recognize how your mind and body are connected and then find and choose new responses to old mental patterns.

Nazi death camp survivor Viktor Frankl provided a good perspective on how this choice is always available to us, even in the direst circumstances: "We who lived in concentration camps can remember the men who walked through the huts comforting others, giving away their last piece of bread... They offer sufficient proof that everything can be taken from a man but one thing: to choose one's attitude in any given set of circumstances, to choose one's own way" (2000, 75). With a wisdom that could not be tortured out of him, or maybe was forged in part by the horrors to which he was subjected, he observed, "Between stimulus and response there is a space. In that space is our power to choose our response. In our response lies our growth and our freedom" (quoted in Pattakos 2008, p. viii).

As you grow in mindfulness, you too may find that you have a choice about how you look at and respond to things, including the things that make you feel anxious. You may also find that you can choose your own way rather then being driven by fear or grasping. This will happen both in your meditation practice and in your day-to-day life. For example, though your first impulse might be to make excuses and flee when your colleagues ask you to join them for lunch, you'll find that you can pause for a moment and turn toward the fearful feeling rather than run away from it. You note fear and anxiety there, in the pit of your stomach, and also the old desire to flee. But in that brief pause you'll also find the space between the stimulus and your response—a space in which you can see that there are other ways you might choose to respond. You may still choose to not join your coworkers, but at least you make this choice consciously and deliberately rather than automatically. Or you may decide to risk joining them to see if you could stay in touch with your body as you sit and eat together. These are the moments in which you discover your growth and your freedom.

a comment about everything

Following the experiences of many people over the years has confirmed for me what has been written about meditation practice for thousands of years: the mind is a chaotic place filled with much internal dialogue and commentary. One student compared her mind to her favorite tea, Constant Comment. Please be aware that this is entirely normal. This is what minds do. My friend Bob Stahl, who practiced mindfulness meditation in a Buddhist monastery for over eight years, taught me that in Buddhist psychology the mind is considered to be one of the sense organs. The eyes see, the ears hear, and the mind thinks. It's just what it does. In a similar vein, Jack Kornfield refers to the mind as a gland that secretes thoughts, just as the salivary glands secrete saliva (Kornfield 2007).

When you practice mindfulness of breathing, you can see that even though thoughts, emotions, and other sensations come and go throughout your practice, the breath also continues to come and go, and you can return to it just by remembering it. Bob Stahl also taught me that in Pali (an ancient Buddhist canonical language) the word for meditation is *bhavana*, which literally means "calling to remember." This remembering is at the heart of being mindful: remembering your intention to stay in the present and beginning again and again when you find you've wandered.

As mentioned, breathing is a convenient link to here and now, as it is always with you and exists only in the present moment. This is particularly important if you're working with anxiety. Because anxiety arises from the mind, returning to the body, and particularly the breath, is a powerful alternative to being swept up in your thoughts and emotions. You may have noticed that when you're anxious, your breath moves up into your chest and becomes more rapid and shallow. When you find this is the case, you can use mindful breathing as discussed in the mindfulness exercise in chapter 1 to help calm your anxiety.

formal and informal mindfulness practice

You can cultivate mindfulness in two principle ways: formally and informally. Formal practice means taking time each day to sit or lie down and invest yourself as much as possible in being present. Throughout this book, you'll have the chance to experience many types of formal practice, such as body scan meditation, sitting meditation, and movement practices like walking meditation and mindful yoga.

Informal practice involves being as present as possible in the moments of your life as you do what you do, from daily tasks to challenging projects. Throughout this book, you will be invited to participate in "See for Yourself" exercises, which are informal mindfulness practices such as the "Eating a Raisin" exercise. These exercises may lead you to explore your daily life in new ways. For example, when eating a meal, you notice the textures, aromas, and colors of one bite of food, feel it as you chew it, and explore the nuances of its flavors. Washing the dishes, you are just washing the dishes and feeling the warmth of the water, the slipperiness of the soap, and every other immediate thing about your experience, including that judgmental thought about your partner, who burned the potatoes and got this impossible crud stuck to the bottom of the pan.

Each of the formal mindfulness practices you'll learn in this book can be adapted for informal practice, providing an opportunity for you to be present wherever you are. In fact, your formal practice supports and informs your informal practice and enables you to actually be here for the experience of your life. For example, you can informally practice listening meditation and walking meditation as you walk in the park or on a busy city street.

Creating a Formal Practice

Establishing a formal practice is the most powerful investment you can make in your life and in your intention to free yourself from shyness, avoidance, and social anxiety. Create a daily schedule for practicing meditation. Use your calendar or another scheduling device to set up a regular time to practice every day. Many people find that one of the best times to practice is early in the morning, before they start their responsibilities for the day.

I recommend having a calendar dedicated solely to your formal practice. You can purchase a calendar for this purpose, write one out by hand, or create one on your computer. If you make a calendar for one week, you can photocopy it and use it again and again. You might even make multiple copies of the schedule for the current week and post it in several places where you'll see it often. When scheduling your practice, be specific, noting the practice you intend to do, the time of day you'll do it, and the duration of your practice. (For a calendar you can download and print out, see my website, www.mindfullivingprograms.com.)

See if you can arrange the place where you do seated meditation to make it optimally comfortable for you. Clear away clutter and make it as simple as possible. You might set a few of your favorite objects nearby to make the space a little friendlier and special to you. Do your best to return to this place and this time every day, even if you can sit only for a few minutes. A few minutes is better than no minutes at all! Know that each minute or even each fraction of a minute you put into this practice is like one of the drops of water falling from the tap of a new well, clearing the channel and opening up a stream of mindfulness in your life.

Informal Practice Through Mindfulness of the Body

Have one meal this week in the same way that you ate the raisin. Turn off all media and phones and eat your meal in silence. Take your time with all of the aspects of eating: seeing your food, smelling it, tasting it, swallowing it. After you finish your meal, take a little while to feel the ongoing experience of the meal: the aftertaste, the warmth, and the way it feels as it moves down into your body.

You can always turn to the body as a place to center and be present, wherever you are. While driving, notice how you're gripping the steering wheel or whether certain parts of your body are tense or tight. Notice how you're breathing, watching the road, and being in your body.

You can practice mindfulness of the body and its sensations in endless situations. While you're walking, notice the feel of each foot touching the earth, the rhythm of your breath, and how it comes into synchrony with the rhythm of your steps. While weeding your garden, see if you can sit comfortably, work at your own pace, and notice every aspect of your experience: the place on the plant where you can get a firm grip on the weed, the way it feels in your hand, the way the roots cling to the earth, and the moment of release as you tug on it. Notice the bugs, the breeze, the scents of the dislodged earth and plants, and the warmth of the sun on your back. However, you don't need a garden for these kinds of experiences; when you are here and now, even the break room at work is a place where you can experience the fullness of life in new ways every day. The library, the grocery store, or even the department of motor vehicles can be a fascinating place, filled with things that are novel and unique. This invitation to practice mindfulness informally in the moments and movements of your life extends to everything you sense and feel in the body. While you are listening, just listen. While you are smelling, just smell. While you are seeing, just see. Practice mindfulness of the body as you wait in line or at a red light, in the shower, as you talk, as you stand up, as you sit down, even as you are reading this sentence right now. Know that anytime you're feeling your senses in your body, you are here and now and in the place of mindfulness. And, of course, you can turn to your breath anytime you like, anywhere you like, and use the sensation of breathing to return to and be in this moment.

schedule practice

Please take a moment now to schedule a daily time for practicing mindfulness of the body. You'll find a convenient mindful practice schedule in the free MPTS workbook at www.mindfullivingprograms.com. A daily practice will serve you best, as it will continue to support you long after you've completed your work with this book.

a calling to remember

The attitudes of mindfulness in this chapter offer gentle guidance for developing your own practice. These suggestions are meant to provide guidelines to support you as you make the practices in this book your own. You'll find that these attitudes are allies that will help you be present for the moments of your life and return to the present when you've become lost in thought or in some well-worn mental rut you've been treading for many years.

In the next chapter, I'll help you deepen your mindfulness practice, become more present in your body, and become more comfortable in the nonverbal world.

4

embracing the
nonverbal world

Out beyond ideas of wrongdoing and rightdoing,
there is a field. I'll meet you there.
When the soul lies down in that grass,
the world is too full to talk about.
Ideas, language. Even the phrase each other
doesn't make any sense.

—Rumi

We live in a world that is dominated by words. We speak and listen, write and read, think and sometimes even dream with words. We're drowning in them. We have devices attached to our ears that allow us to speak and listen to words in almost any circumstance. As a result, we no longer think people walking down the street talking to themselves are nuts, because often a good number of the people we see on the street are talking out loud to someone who isn't physically there. We've become the nuts who can't stop talking. There are few moments in our lives when we're free from the tyranny of words, because even when we aren't talking, texting, reading, listening, e-mailing, or otherwise engaging with words out there in the world, we're talking and listening to ourselves in our heads.

This chapter sings the praises of the nonverbal world and will offer you a variety of ways that you can go there to visit or even live for a while.

the body as refuge

Social anxiety is essentially created and perpetuated by the words in our heads about ourselves and other people. Anxiety feeds on the things we say to ourselves and therefore requires frequent verbal maintenance to keep regenerating itself. But what if we found ways to shut up, even for a little while? What if we put more of our energy into awareness rather than critical thoughts and stopped feeding the flames of anxiety with more and more words? These are questions that you can answer for yourself when you literally come to your senses in the nonverbal world. You may find, as so many others have, that bringing all your attention into the body starves anxiety and puts a damper on its flames.

At its heart, this is what mindfulness meditation is: an investment in nondiscursive awareness, in putting words aside and feeding the part of your mind that thrives in the nonverbal world. Mindfulness *is* nondiscursive awareness. It emerges when you are actually here, in this moment, without being consumed by words, concepts, and judgments. It emerges in those moments when you're no longer identified with the thinker or the talker within. Awareness is an overarching mental faculty that is much larger than words and operates without them.

This is why meditation retreats are usually conducted in what is called "noble silence." Participants may also be asked to abstain from reading or writing over the time of the retreat. You might think that spending days or even weeks living closely with a group of people without words would feel profoundly alienating, but it's often exactly the opposite—the silence fosters a feeling of being deeply and intimately connected with the people you share this experience with. This connectedness flourishes even when participants make minimal or no eye contact and don't converse. Curiously enough, it seems that when we suspend our principle ways of trying to connect with others, we can actually feel more connected.

When you are in the nonverbal world, not only can you be more completely who you are with yourself, you can actually feel more free to be who you are with others. In the absence of words, you no longer have to express yourself well, listen well, or worry about how you want to be seen or don't want to be seen. Of course, all of this is well-known to anyone who is shy. This is why shy folks love nature, their pets, listening to music, and so many other things that don't involve having to use words. Freedom from words also brings freedom from a great deal of performance anxiety.

Because a huge portion of all anxiety arises from thoughts constructed from words, particularly self-critical words, you can be free from anxiety in moments when you're fully in your body and not in your mind. In this way, the body becomes a refuge, a kind of sanctuary from the self-blame and self-doubt so often churned out by the thinking mind. This is also why the body or awareness of sensations is a traditional place for meditation practice to begin.

When you invest yourself in direct sensory experience and spend time in the nonverbal world of your body, you begin to experience the world in heightened ways. This can happen anytime you quiet your mind and come to your senses—whether running or sitting still, and whether sitting in your car or sitting on a meditation cushion. When you are actually here, paying attention to what's before you, the whole world seems to come alive, even sometimes full of magic and splendor. Something as simple as a spiderweb glistening in the sun can become an exquisite work of art when you are here to witness it.

• Discoveries on the Path: *Frank's Story*

Frank, who owned a successful but stressful business, participated in a mindfulness-based stress reduction program to gain some skill in managing the stress which was threatening his health. As the class progressed into the sixth week, he couldn't help comparing his progress with that of his classmates and feeling a little disappointed. Several classmates had shared personal discoveries from their meditation practice that had helped them make important changes in their lives, but it seemed to Frank that he was still stuck in the same old rut in which he started the program. At the end of that class, he only half-jokingly said, "Maybe I'm just a hopeless case!"

Frank came to his seventh class smiling and exuberant. He'd had an experience he couldn't wait to share. That morning he'd realized that he actually was showing up for and appreciating more of the moments of his life. This realization hit him

70

as he was waiting in his car at a drive-through eatery. Startled by the car behind him honking, Frank was astonished to see that he had become so transfixed by the beauty and symmetry of a spiderweb on a bush that he had forgotten all about being in his car in line. In the "go, go, go" mind-set he'd developed in recent years, he normally would have been fixated on how slowly the line seemed to be progressing, how much time was passing, how much he had to do, how he couldn't afford to be waiting around like this, and so on. Being completely caught up in the moment was something that hadn't happened to him since he was a child, and he loved it. He had slipped into the nonverbal world for a few moments.

The world we experience without words often calls forth fond memories of times when bugs and leaves and even water standing in puddles could fill us with fascination and appreciation for the sheer magic in this world—a magic most of us forget as we enter into the world of discursive thought and responsibilities. With this sensibility, frost crystals on the window dazzle your senses and even your breath coming and going can seem like a delicious meal. When you're present in your body rather than in your thoughts, you can feel and notice things that escape the rational mind. Many people who do body-oriented, sensation-based meditation practices for the first time report experiencing feelings that they haven't had since early childhood.

As you proceed, don't expect that mindfulness practice will dispel the words in your head. The fact is, it's likely to make them even more obvious to you. Meditation isn't about stopping your thoughts; it's about changing the degree of your investment in them. Every human being has faced the impossibility of stopping thoughts at one time or another, particularly when lying in bed at night before some major life event. Stopping your thoughts isn't the intention of meditation practice; the intention is to relate to your thoughts differently. This is why staying in touch with your body is such a powerful ally in mindfulness practice. It provides a place to center your awareness and offers restful moments of freedom from critical thinking. For example, from the perspective of presence in the belly, with the breath, you can witness thoughts come and go and choose not to get that involved in them. They haven't stopped, you're just letting them be.

As discussed, feeling shy often means being critical of yourself and then imagining that everyone else views you in the same critical way. When you look at yourself from the perspective of the critic, your appearance or performance can seem to define your value as a human being. A useful antidote is to shift into the experiential mode of taking in sensory information and feeling the body from the inside out, rather than looking at it and thinking about it from some imaginary perspective outside of yourself. From the inside you don't even feel a body per se, you feel things like warmth or coolness, movement or stillness, roughness or smoothness. You hear the clock ticking or the air conditioner coming on. You notice the weight of your hands on your lap. These things are. You are.

You've already begun practicing this kind of nonverbal presence during conscious breathing and by eating mindfully. When you bring your full attention to things like the breath coming and going and you sense its coolness, its warmth, its depth, and its rhythm, you enter into the peace of the nonverbal world. The following body scan is a perfect way to deepen your awareness of the nonverbal world.

mindfulness practice:
Body Scan Meditation

This practice, in which you bring a great deal of attention to the body, is a powerful way to cultivate mindfulness and build concentration. Slowly, region by region, you focus as closely as you can on the sensations you feel as you scan. As you bring your attention to each part of your body, you'll notice many things. You may find yourself feeling worried about some parts of your body and critical of others. You may find yourself recoiling from pain or dropping into heavy and compelling sleepiness. You're also likely to find that the mind seems to have a comment and judgment about everything. Acknowledge these things and let them be. This is normal. In fact, one of the benefits of this practice is that you can learn a lot about your mind and its habitual ways of looking at things. The intention is to acknowledge what the mind has to say, then return to the body and the immediate sensations of being present.

A good time to practice the body scan is when you feel rested and alert, like after you have just awakened in the morning. Do this practice lying down on the floor on a mat or pad that offers some cushion for your body but isn't so soft that it will make you feel sleepy. If this is extremely uncomfortable, you can do the body scan in bed, but try to be well rested so you aren't likely to fall asleep. As mindfulness practice is about waking up and growing in awareness, you might set an intention to sit up and open your eyes if you find yourself drowsing off. Choose a place that's comfortable and quiet where you won't be disturbed for at least thirty-five minutes.

Read the instructions thoroughly, then lie down and direct your attention into your body. Because most people prefer to listen to the instructions as they practice the body scan, you might consider making a recording of the instructions, or buying a recorded version (see Resources) to play when you practice. Turn off any music or other media that might draw you out of your felt sense of your body. As you direct your attention upward through your body, take your time and linger a little while in every part of your body, especially those parts where you're experiencing any discomfort or pain.

You may notice that this practice doesn't include instructions about relaxing your body. This isn't the goal of practice, although most people do indeed discover various degrees of relaxation in the body scan. The goal is to be mindful. In this practice, please attend to your body with a tender curiosity. See if you can linger at the painful or contracted places and care for them with kindness and compassion. Remember, the intention isn't to push away but to be with, not to control but to allow. See if you can practice acceptance with whatever you encounter.

1. Lie on your back with your legs slightly apart and your feet falling out. Open your palms to the ceiling if this is comfortable for you, and feel your body settle into place. As you take your place on your mat, consider that you are giving a gift to yourself and extend some appreciation to yourself for creating this time to grow in mindfulness.

2. Notice where your body is being supported by the mat, the floor, and ultimately the earth beneath you. Feel into the places that are bearing the most weight or calling for the most attention. As you sense into the body as a whole and notice what you notice, see if there are places that feel more tense than others and breathe into those places with curiosity and kindness. See if they're calling for some

shift in your position or directing your attention to release whatever is being held there. It may be that this is just a tense area, and if that is so, let it be as it is and continue to settle into place.

3. Bringing your attention into your abdominal region, notice that as you breathe in, the belly rises, and as you breathe out, it descends once again toward the backbone. If it's helpful, place one hand lightly on the belly to assist you in feeling the rising and falling. Let the breath come and go as it will and breathe without effort or trying to change the breath in any way. Notice you don't have to make it happen; it happens all on its own. Allow your attention to settle entirely into the sensations of the breath coming in and the breath going out, and use this felt sense of the breath as your way to show up and be present. As the body scan proceeds, you can direct your breath into any region of the body. See if you can feel the breath move into or fill that area. If this doesn't seem to fit for you, just maintain a sense of the breath coming and going and let this rhythm guide you gently through each and every part of the body.

4. When you're ready, release your attention from the belly. If you brought your hand to your belly, return it to the side of your body. Directing your attention into the region of your left foot, notice whatever you sense there. Without wiggling or tensing or physically doing anything at all with the foot, bring your awareness into each toe, with a friendly and curious attention to each sensation. Perhaps you do not even feel a sensation; that's fine too. Let everything you notice just be as it is, being with it in a kind, sensitive way. Being present with your left foot and letting yourself be.

5. As you have noticed with your mindful breathing practice, your mind may wander from the body from time to time. When that happens, bring the same tender and compassionate attention to your thoughts as you did when practicing mindful breathing. Perhaps a few moments of inquiry are called for. A little curiosity about the nature of your mind's wanderings can sometimes be revealing and helpful. Then let it be and redirect your attention back into the

body. Returning to the present moment and beginning again. Feeling into the region of your body you're focused on as if for the first time.

6. Notice the top of the foot, the sole, the heel, and each side. If you feel no sensation in any region, that's okay. Many people notice regions of nonsensation as they do the body scan. If you notice something that hurts, you might just acknowledge it with the phrase "unpleasant sensation," or if you find a pleasant sensation you might note "pleasant sensation." Feeling nothing or very little in any region, you might acknowledge "neutral sensation." Notice whatever you notice and let yourself be.

7. Notice the difference between thoughts about anything you encounter and the direct, felt sensation as you now slowly and mindfully direct your attention up into your ankle and then explore, as you did with the foot, everything that makes up this marvelous joint we call ankle. Drop beneath the envelope of the skin, if you like, to feel into the joint itself, the tendons, the nerves, the blood vessels. Then, as you are ready, bring this same quality of attention into every region of your left leg, taking your time and exploring, with awareness and nonjudgment, everything there is to notice in your left leg: the lower leg, the knee, and the thigh all the way up to where the leg meets the hip. At that point, breathe in and out for a few breaths and be present with the whole left leg.

8. Next, release your attention from the left leg and direct it into to your right foot, exploring everything you can in this part of your body. Then explore each and every part of your right leg in the same way you did with your left leg, being present, curious and kind.

9. Continue scanning upward in your body, directing this kind and curious awareness through your pelvis and genitals, buttocks, belly, chest, and back. See if you can be inclusive of everything you encounter in your body and in the moments of this practice—the pleasant sensations, the unpleasant sensations, the stories and judgments that come

up in different regions of your body. Letting yourself be. Letting everything be.

10. Next, bring your attention to the left hand and arm, attending to your fingers, thumb, wrist, lower arm, elbow, and upper arm with friendly receptivity.

11. Direct your attention to your right hand and arm in the same way.

12. Release your attention from your right arm and bring it into the shoulders, neck, head, and face. Notice how your face feels in this place of nonjudging awareness, where you don't need to make any kind of appearance, where you don't need to express anything, hide anything, or impress anyone. Notice the experience of your lips, tongue, teeth, nostrils, eyes, ears, and the top and back of your head. Being present with each part, without judgment and without striving.

13. When you have scanned your entire body, bring your attention to embrace your body from the top of your head to the tips of your toes. Acknowledge your wholeness and completeness. Notice what it feels like to be fully embodied and fully present. Spend some time here and just let yourself be.

14. Thank yourself for giving yourself this mindfulness practice. Know that this is a gift of loving-kindness.

Many people are so sleep deprived and on the go that they begin to drowse as soon as they settle into the body scan. This is normal, and sometimes the most compassionate thing you can do is just allow yourself to sleep. Know that this is perfectly okay too. This practice isn't meant to be a rigid discipline, but an expression of self-caring and self-loving. Be kind to yourself and sleep if your body needs it. When you awaken, try the body scan again. If falling asleep continues to be a problem with this practice, you might try doing it after you've had a good night of sleep, or do it while sitting up or even standing up. Also, bring the same kind of compassionate inquiry into the sleepiness. Sleepiness isn't always about fatigue; sometimes it's a way to avoid facing things that you don't feel ready to face. Because mindfulness is about self-compassion, as well as waking up and growing in wide-open awareness and attention, with practice you'll gradually increase in wakefulness, and in the courage to see what you need to see and feel what you need to feel.

Notes to Yourself

Take a little time to write in your journal about your body scan. Note the ways your mind wandered from the practice at any given moment and what you did to work with it. Also note how you feel in your body and mind after doing the body scan.

• Discoveries on the Path: *Beverly's Story*

Beverly signed up for a mindfulness-based stress reduction program to help herself with extremely painful abdominal symptoms due to irritable bowel syndrome. On the day of her first class, her symptoms were so severe that she almost didn't come. But remembering the advice of her physician, she decided to try to do what she could.

As we began the body scan, Beverly began to cry and then sob. It was so rare for her to be with her body and her feelings that all of the unacknowledged grief and despair she felt about this debilitating condition completely overwhelmed her. She cried and sobbed throughout the practice. As often happens when someone in class drops into such anguish, it called forth sadness and sobs from several other participants.

When Beverly came up to me after class, she wanted to tell me what had happened to her. She was a little embarrassed about her outpouring, but even more, she was astonished that by the time the practice was completed, she wasn't feeling any discomfort in her gut. This gushing release of her deep sadness helped her realize for the first time that this unhappiness was somehow related to her IBS symptoms. She wondered about the many tears she had swallowed over the years to "be strong," and she left with a powerful insight and an intention to open to her feelings more.

I marveled at her realization. This was a rare and extraordinary experience from a first-time meditation practice. But my surprises for the evening weren't over. A few minutes later, another woman came up to talk with me about her tears during class and told me very nearly the same thing. She too suffered from IBS pain and had an experience much like Beverly's. As she left, I wondered how many of us hurt ourselves by not feeling our feelings because we don't want to accept them.

When you begin the practice of mindfulness meditation, you step into a place where you may make powerful discoveries about your life, the things that scare or hurt you, and the things that cause stress in your life. You bring light into dark places, some of them long unilluminated. There's no certainty as to what you may find there in your own disowned places, but it's likely that your efforts to avoid exploring and being with yourself in these places have had consequences in your body or in your life. It's a huge commitment to be with yourself like this. Know that this is an act of great love and great courage.

traveling in the forest at night

I live in a forest in northern California where we don't have streetlights or sidewalks, and, back when I moved here many years ago, we had no roads. We lived in small cabins, teepees, and domes connected by narrow forest paths that stretched as long as a mile between homes. Traveling on those paths at night was often an adventure.

Rather than spending money on batteries for flashlights, we made "can candles," similar to small lanterns, that we could carry to illuminate the paths. These primitive contraptions weren't reliable and frequently went out or fell apart altogether, leaving you alone in a vast and dark forest, unable to see the path. We learned that this was okay if you would just stand there a minute or two, settle down, and really feel into the place where you were standing. This feel of the earth could take you home. From that moment on, you'd pay very close attention to each step. Surprisingly, even your ears could help you find your way. The moment you stepped slightly off the path, you'd not only feel a new roughness under your feet, you'd hear yourself crunching the leaves and dry grasses. There was a smoothness and a silence on the path that disappeared the moment you veered from it and reappeared the moment you returned to it. Since you knew where this path led, if you took one slow step after another, you would eventually reach your destination. The secret lay in paying attention to the path, one step at a time.

walking meditation

One of the common mind and body experiences that accompanies anxiety is the feeling of agitation. When you feel agitated, it can be excruciating to try to sit or lie still. The body begs for movement, even extreme movement, like running or intensive exercise. Know that mindfulness need not be practiced only when you're at rest; you can also practice mindfulness while moving. Sometimes the wisest and kindness choice is to listen to what the body is asking for and honor its needs. If feelings like agitation are extremely compelling, bring walking into your meditation, using the practices below. After you walk for a while, the body and mind will settle down enough to enable you to experience mindfulness while in motion.

mindfulness practice:
Narrow-Gauge Walking Meditation

This is a different kind of walking than most of us are used to; it's walking to be fully where you are rather than to get somewhere else. I call this narrow-gauge practice because the intention is to narrow your focus to simple details of walking, such as the sensation of a foot lifting, moving, and once again making contact with the earth and then supporting the weight of the body as you lift the other foot. As you are walking, you're just walking—just taking this one step and feeling the earth beneath this foot in this moment.

To begin, give yourself about thirty minutes for this practice and choose a place where you can create a lane about fifteen feet long in which to walk back and forth. Standing in your lane, settle into your sense of here and now and find your balance over your feet. If you're comfortable doing so, close your eyes for a moment to better feel the sensation of your feet pressing into the ground and supporting your body. See if you can stay closely attuned to this sensation of the feet making contact with the earth as you proceed in your walking practice.

Opening your eyes, lift one foot, then take a small step forward. Notice the sensations involved in lifting your foot, moving it forward, and then placing it back onto the earth. Feel your body shift as you bring your weight onto that foot and then begin lifting and placing the other foot another small step ahead of you. Feel the body's weight shifting onto that foot, being present for the sensation of the foot touching the earth.

Allow your body to be at ease, and have a sense of dignity in your posture. It's not necessary to watch your feet, but it is helpful to stay in touch with the felt sensation of each step. The eyes can be cast slightly down and a little ahead of you with a soft gaze at the ground. As you reach the end of the path, stop and stand still a moment or two, then turn and face the other end of your lane, noticing your choice to turn to the right or to the left to get into this position. Pause a moment before slowly and mindfully walking back to where you started, aware of lifting and placing your feet and shifting your weight.

Some people find that coordinating their breathing with their steps helps them be more present in each step. Some feel they keep a better sense of balance if the steps are quite small. Some need to move quite slowly, and others feel best if they're moving more quickly. Listen to your body and move with your own rhythm and presence.

Notes to Yourself

Take some time write in your journal about your walking meditation practice. What did you notice as you walked with this much awareness of each step and each moment? What was it like to be this attentive to walking itself rather than some destination?

mindfulness practice:
Broad-Gauge Walking Meditation

Here's another option for walking meditation that can also help you cultivate mindfulness. I call it broad-gauge walking practice because it's more informal and expansive. It's good to begin the practice of walking meditation with the narrow-gauge instructions above and spend much time there, perhaps many hours of practice, before you implement this broad-gauge walking meditation. You might consider beginning this broader practice only after you've found it possible to remain in touch with each moment in the narrow-gauge practice.

Once you're ready, begin the narrow-gauge process as above, then accelerate your pace, walking faster if you like and expanding or broadening your attention to take in more of your experience as you walk. In this mindful movement practice you may walk any distance, anywhere, at any speed that feels right for you. You can even run if you want to. The principal instruction is the same as in narrow-gauge practice: to be fully present in each moment you are walking rather than consumed with mind chatter. In broad-gauge practice you are also invited to be open to the experience of the environment in which you're moving. In this practice you're more open to notice things such as the way clouds are forming over the mountains nearby or how the sunlight is glistening in the snow-covered meadow you're crossing. The invitation is to turn toward whatever calls your attention and be with it as long as you like, stopping if you want to take a closer look or to listen more intently. Remember, the overarching intention is to be mindful, to be in this experience of the now with nondiscursive awareness.

This practice isn't intended to replace the more formal and restrictive narrow-gauge walking practice, but to give you another option to experience mindfulness in movement. You may like to make this kind of walking practice part of a regular exercise program, allowing you to grow in strength and cardiovascular health as well as mindfulness. All of these benefits will be helpful in working with anxiety or depression.

Notes to Yourself

Take some time to write in your journal about this broader experience of walking meditation. What did you notice about your environment? What did you notice about your thoughts, your emotions, and your body?

becoming an observer

As you continue to take steps to build your mindfulness practice, you'll soon find a part of you that's witnessing yourself sense, think, and feel things. This aspect of self goes by many names, including the internal observer and the observer self. When walking alone in the forest at night, you notice not only your steps, but also thoughts and emotions, such as "What if I can't find the cabin and have to spend the night out here?" and "Why can't I figure out how make these stupid can candles work right? I hate these damn things!" You also notice that getting swept up in thoughts and feelings distracts you from your steps altogether. As a result, you can stray from the path for several steps without noticing it. This can be a genuine hazard in the forest; if you get lost due to distracting thoughts, it can take a long time to find your way again.

This is where your internal observer, the dispassionate witness of your consciousness, can help you. From this part of your mind, you can observe when you're getting lost in a mental quagmire and return your attention to the immediacy of each step. The internal observer is the part of your mind that notices as you stray into self-doubt and self-criticism and therefore can gently remind you to return to the immediacy of seeing, hearing, and otherwise sensing the present moment. It can remind you that thoughts are just thoughts, that they come and they go and you don't have to get involved with them unless you want to. Anxious thoughts and feelings are temporary, after all, and generally lead to nowhere but trouble.

The internal observer helps you stay in touch with your body and the moment and can help you find your way through difficult mental states. It is the nonstriving, nondiscursive awareness that you cultivate in mindfulness practice and that simply witnesses what's happening without judgment or efforts to change or suppress anything. It's a dispassionate witness to your thoughts, emotions, and actions and operates in being mode, not doing mode.

Shifting to the perspective of the observer self from time to time helps you take things off of automatic and live your life more deliberately. This self-witnessing is like shining a light into the habits of your mind and gives you a measure of choice about how you look at things. Making the unconscious more conscious is a tremendous benefit of mindfulness—and also of psychotherapy.

As you become more familiar with the internal observer, you'll realize that it has always been with you. You've known in it in dreams, and perhaps even during traumatic events, as the part of you that is dispassionately observing you.

see for yourself exercise 2:
The Internal Observer

The internal observer is that faculty of your awareness that can witness your thoughts, emotions, sensations, behaviors without judgment or attachment. It's the clear awareness that emerges when you aren't acting from some agenda and can be fully present with things as they are. As you invest more time in this simple, wide-open kind of awareness, you can sometimes get insights into the entrancing trickery of your small self—that part of yourself that is always chasing after or trying to hang onto pleasant feelings and, with the same tenacity, doing everything it can to avoid unpleasant feelings.

Over the next week, see if you can turn to the observer self whenever you notice you've become caught in either the tug of desire or the escape reflex of avoidance. It might be something as simple as a craving for a mocha or as overwhelming as an invitation from a person you're attracted to. Rather than being possessed by or totally focused on the thing that you want or would like to escape from, take a few moments to notice what's happening in your body as you experience these compulsions of desire or avoidance. Notice what's triggered this urge in you and what thoughts and emotions you are having. When you can, take a few minutes to write in your shyness journal about your experience and what you noticed in your mind and body.

These are the habits of mind and behavior that can get you lost in your shyness patterns and keep you there. So the more you can illuminate them, the more you may be able to uncouple from some of these automatic reactions. You may notice how your reactions to certain thoughts and feelings can be so automatic that, once you experience them, your choices and behaviors are predictable. The internal observer can dispel the trances of desire and fear and help you not fall under their spell again. As you work with your shyness and social anxiety, you'll find that being able to shift into your observer self will help you in the same ways it can help you on a narrow forest path at night.

Another way to get glimpses of your internal observer is in your dreams, especially if you affirm an intention to do so before you go to sleep and just as you awaken in the morning. To get a sense of this extraordinary faculty, simply remind yourself to look for and acknowledge that part of your consciousness that's simply witnessing you do whatever you do in your dreams. With some reflection in the morning, you may discover that there is a part of you that was the actor in your dream and another part of you that was watching you act in the dream. Take a little time in the morning to write in your shyness journal about whatever you discover.

In the dream state, we rarely consider "which me is me," but upon awakening this differentiation can be quite puzzling: "If I was the person who was watching myself fly over campus, than who was the person who was flying?" This can be an equally curious riddle when you're practicing mindfulness meditation and notice your thoughts coming and going: "If I'm watching thoughts come and go, who's thinking? If I'm watching self-judgments come and go, who's the judge?"

see for yourself exercise 3:
Mindfulness of Hearing

As you come to the end of your next mindful breathing or body scan practice, please spend at least ten minutes with the intention to be fully present for hearing. Notice what sounds come to you and employ each and every sound as your way of being present in the same way you have employed each and every sensation of the breath or body. Notice the difference between the sensation of sound and the thoughts, interpretations, and judgments about what you hear.

Then, over the next week, create a little time each day to be as present as possible with what you hear. Notice the sounds that are distant from you and the sounds that are close to you. The world around you can come alive in very interesting ways when you listen without judgment or preferences. Even something you might think of as mundane or unpleasant, like the sounds in a subway or the amazing cacophony of a bustling city, can take on a whole new flavor when you listen to it from mindfulness. Feast on sound in the forest, by the sea, and everywhere you find yourself, in the early morning, late at night, and whenever you can. This will lay an important foundation for work we'll do later in the book, where listening mindfully will play an integral part in interpersonal mindfulness practices. For now, know that mindfulness of hearing is a very powerful meditation practice.

schedule practice

Please take a moment now to schedule a daily time for practicing mindfulness with the body scan and mindful walking. It will serve you best to practice every day, perhaps alternating the two practices from day to day.

a calling to remember

This chapter is a bit of a mind-bender, really: me writing with words and you reading these words about the beauty and power of the nonverbal world! Of course, we need these words to share a common experience that is much more than words. It can never be adequately captured by words, yet these words and the exercises they describe are a useful tool for helping you discover a more mindful experience of living.

Being able to sit without words reveals a world that's extraordinary in every sense of the word. Very young children live in this world of seeing things for the first time, and from time to time we adults can recapture this sense of seeing things freshly, as if for the first time. Mindfulness brings more of this awareness into our lives. Trees and clouds and breezes, and even the sensations of simply breathing, become exquisite when we're awake in the nonverbal world. This is why staying in touch with your body and your senses is such a powerful ally in your practice. The body is a place where you center your awareness and find refuge from critical thoughts. Turning to your senses can enable you to be fully present in the here and now.

Now that you've established a foundation of mindfulness practice and have started to make contact with the nonverbal world, you're in a good position to start directing your practice to your thoughts and emotions. In the next chapter, we'll explore how you can bring your growing mindfulness to the specific attitudes of mind and behavior that create shyness.

Part III

caring for yourself mindfully

This being human is a guesthouse.
Every morning a new arrival.

A joy, a depression, a meanness,
some momentary awareness comes
as an unexpected visitor.

Welcome and entertain them all!
Even if they're a crowd of sorrows,
who violently sweep your house
empty of its furniture,
still, treat each guest honorably.
He may be clearing you out
for some new delight.

The dark thought, the shame, the malice,
meet them at the door laughing,
and invite them in.

Be grateful for whoever comes,
because each has been sent
as a guide from beyond.

—Rumi, "The Guest House"

5

you are not your thoughts

We don't see things the way they are, we see things the way we are.

—The Talmud

Gloria decided that she needed to do something with her hair, so she splurged at one of the best hair salons in town. The next morning as she talked with her boss at work, she saw a couple of her coworkers looking her way and laughing and felt totally humiliated. She wondered how they could be so mean. She thought her hair looked nice until she saw their reaction; then she felt totally self-conscious and hated it and just wanted to hide. She thought they were cruel and decided she wouldn't be friendly with them any more. Later, at a break, one of the women came into the break room and sat down with Gloria. As they sipped some coffee, her coworker smiled and said she liked Gloria's new "do." She said she thought it was very flattering to the shape of her face and that the color really went well with her skin tone. Then she asked Gloria what she thought about their boss's new toupee. Gloria suddenly realized they hadn't been laughing at *her* hair, but at his. In just that moment her mood lifted and she liked her hair again.

For good and ill, our thoughts are interwoven into our lives, and how we respond to our thoughts can create a great deal of emotional chaos for us and often for the people around us. We can bring that which we fear most upon ourselves simply by worrying that it's going to happen. For example, if you invest enough worry into the fear that you'll blush and sweat at the "surprise" birthday party your coworkers are planning for you, you can be sure that you'll be red as a beet and drenched with sweat. But if you can create a little distance between yourself and your thoughts and learn to examine these creative narratives as mental events rather than facts of reality, you can begin to dismantle some of the personal narratives that create so much anxiety.

Nothing can cause quite so much trouble as an unexamined mind. The importance of being mindful of thought has been expressed in countless ways throughout history and is found in some form or another in the sacred texts of many of the world's religions. However, none of us need to read these things in scriptures or textbooks to accept their validity. We can scarcely go a day or even an hour without creating narratives about ourselves and the world and reacting to them as if they were fact.

the power of thought

As awareness grows, we discover that a huge portion of our lives is constructed with thoughts. With our thoughts we make the world—and ourselves. This is one of the central concepts of cognitive psychology, and in meditation practice you can see this for yourself. We tell ourselves stories about ourselves—a lot—and much of the time we live in the tales that we spin. In our stories, we have certain concepts about ourselves and the world, and we actually impose them on what we experience. For example, we may view some people as "legends in their own minds" and others as "complete idiots" and then discover that our experiences pretty much conform with what we expect. It's not that the world conforms to what we want or don't want. It's just that each of us makes of it whatever we expect to make of it. Like Gloria, we don't see things as they are, but as we interpret them. We then live within those interpretations as if they were real.

Our interpretations can be surprisingly powerful, coloring our world and even determining how we feel about the image we see looking back at us in the mirror. Our interpretations are composed of expectations, fears, and desires that *will* distort our thoughts. I saw a bumper sticker recently that said, "Don't believe everything you think!" This is a useful piece of advice that reminds us how tricky our very own thoughts can be. When I felt extremely shy, I could look into the mirror of others' eyes and, no matter who they were or how they actually felt, decide they were looking at me critically.

challenging thoughts

Thoughts may not always reflect reality, but they are still essential and powerful tools. One of life's great challenges is learning to listen to thoughts with clarity and discernment and without being taken over or deluded by them. Cognitive psychology and meditation are both ways to awaken the mind to the mind itself and find the truth within the thoughts and interpretations through which we form our perceptions of the world.

We usually believe the mind's hype, particularly if it's repeated often enough. Mindfulness gives us a perspective from which to witness our thoughts and defuse the compelling power they have in our lives. With mindfulness, we can spend time with a thought before we act on it or even believe it. Teacher and author Byron Katie (2002) offers four helpful questions for working with particular thoughts:

1. Is it true?

2. Can you absolutely know that it's true?

3. How do you react when you believe that thought?

4. Who would you be without that thought?

It's worthwhile to challenge thoughts in this way. You may be surprised by the sheer number of thoughts you have that simply aren't true, and even more surprised at how they can flood you with powerful emotions nonetheless.

So how does this relate to shyness? The shyness identity is also constructed with thoughts. It's a self pasted together with labels, concepts, judgments, generalizations from past experiences, and projections of future possibilities. It's something you experience—not what you are. Just finding ways to step outside of your thoughts and investigate them without identifying with them or trying to push them away is a powerful practice that can help break their spell. Because the part of you that's looking at and exploring the role of your perceptions and interpretations isn't swept up in them, you can begin to see your particular way of creating your world. When you stop identifying with that creation, you're more able to respond to the world freely.

follow that thought

Here's a step-by-step outline of one way we cognitively create our self-concept and personality:

1. Thoughts arise.

2. Thoughts give rise to emotions.

3. Emotions give rise to moods.

4. Moods harden into personality.

5. Personality hardens into habits of behavior.

6. Habits of behavior gradually shape the body.

Thus, the body can become an expression of a person's history. Look into the faces of people who have lived a long time. Sometimes their faces tell a vivid story of the mental and emotional states that have dominated their lives. Worry lines can reveal a lifetime of anxiety, while crow's-feet and other smile wrinkles can reveal a lifetime of laughter.

You can see for yourself how this process works by imagining that you've just done something very embarrassing in front of a group of people. Or even better, remember an embarrassing event from your past (pick a good one). Attend to the details of that scenario as best you can and stay with it until a feeling of embarrassment comes over you. Mentally exaggerate everything if you need to. As soon as you feel embarrassed, notice what's going on with your body.

If you were able to bring up feelings of embarrassment or shame, you probably noticed that this affected your body in some way. Your thoughts can bring up emotions that affect your body. If you imagine these kinds of things a lot, the resulting emotions can create a mood, and once a mood has come over you, you may be in its grip for hours or even days.

Moods tend to have a selective memory process attached to them and can bring up memories of other times you've felt that way, including feeling humiliated. Likewise, they can leave you barely able to remember times when you felt differently. If you return to a mood often enough and live in it long enough, it will gradually define your personality. It will also take shape in your body as mannerisms and physical reactions. In the case of shyness, that might include such things as blushing, sweating, a faster heartbeat, and shallower, faster breath. The good news is, you can also make use of these very same physical responses as a sort of biofeedback system. When you feel sensations of embarrassment, it can be a cue that you're thinking about being embarrassed. Being mindful of your body can give you clues about emotional and mental states, and this is a valuable resource.

• Discoveries on the Path: *Teri's Story*

Teri reported an important personal discovery to her meditation group. She told them about a recent meditation practice in which she found her lips tight and cramped. She decided to leave them that way for a few moments to feel into why they were so tightly pursed. She discovered that she hadn't been present at all during most of her practice up to that point. Instead, she had been mentally reviewing a painful event from the previous day. She had met her friend Beth at a restaurant for lunch and called her Bev a couple of times. She didn't even notice her error until her friend told her. Ruminating about this during her meditation, she felt stupid and angry at herself. By feeling into the tension in her lips, she realized that they were pursed due to her anger, and that her anger was related to the self-critical and self-blaming story she was telling herself. She announced to the group that her lips had become her "canary in the coal mine," and that she was going to use any tightness she found there as a clue to what was happening in her often self-critical mind.

By paying attention to your body, you may become familiar with physical expressions of emotions that can lead you back to the thoughts that prompted them, as Teri did. A simple insight such as hers can provide enough illumination to break the whole cascade of thought, emotion, mood, and behavior. This can even have physical benefits. In Teri's case, she later told me that this discovery not only helped her with habitual self-critical ruminations, it also essentially eliminated a problem she'd had with mouth and jaw pain. We're all different, so you have to look for your own indicators. You may notice something like a tight jaw connected to angry thoughts or tight shoulders due to self-blame. Recognizing and identifying physical sensations or behaviors associated with different thoughts can help you learn to work more consciously and deliberately with thoughts that cause trouble. Then you can short-circuit the process before you're entirely entranced into the fear body.

thoughts that create anxiety

In cognitive therapy, the term *cognitive distortions* is used to refer to certain types of thoughts that give rise to emotional problems. In therapy groups, they often get the more user-friendly name "stinking thinking." The defining characteristic of stinking thinking is confusing problematic thoughts with reality and then patterning our behavior according to them. It's a simple case of garbage in, garbage out. There are many different kinds of anxiety-generating thoughts that are characteristic of the painfully shy. Let's look at a few recognized troublemakers: time traveling, catastrophizing, self-judgment, feelings of inadequacy, and projections of self-criticism.

Time Traveling

Mark Twain is reported to have once said, "I've been through some terrible things in my life, some of which actually happened!"

A surefire way to feed anxiety is by anticipating the future and imagining the disasters that may lie ahead. Looking into the future, you can suffer humiliations and defeats that haven't even happened, and if you replay these thoughts, you can end up suffering an imaginary event many times. Or you can travel in the other direction and make yourself even more miserable as you look back in time and relive whatever you may have suffered in the past, and then imaginatively travel into the future to live it again and again. Anticipation of the future is what generates anxiety. If you habitually live with fearful thoughts about the future, you can be reasonably assured that your anxieties will grow and multiply. Sometimes this is called "future tripping." It's like

Miracle-Gro for anxiety, which explains why anxiety is often paired with the word "anticipatory," as in anticipatory anxiety. If you review anticipated disasters again and again, you can water this seed of anxiety into a regular nightmare.

Catastrophizing

In most anxiety conditions, anticipation is paired with *catastrophizing*. This is a form of pessimism or biased reasoning in which you assume that your negative interpretations or expectations represent the way things are or will be. For example, you can screen out positive expressions on people's faces and focus on negative expressions, and then imagine that those frowns represent a negative judgment about you—and that everyone judges you in this way. Or before a big presentation at work, you can imagine that you're going to forget all of the things you rehearsed for weeks and see yourself bumbling and speechless in front of the big boss. You may be more familiar with catastrophizing in the form of belief in Murphy's Law—"Anything that can go wrong will go wrong."

Self-Judgment

One of the most ruthless ways of getting lost and stuck in shyness and social anxiety is with negative self-judgments. Through the lens of these self-judgments, you may imagine yourself as separate from, and worse than, everyone else. Sometimes self-judgment cloaks itself in the guise of "constructive self-criticism" that offers you ways to improve yourself. But if you really pay attention to this type of internal commentary, you may find that it's often simply destructive self-judgment in disguise. If you listen to this internal commentary enough, you end up creating a negative bias against yourself, and many other thoughts will arrange themselves to reflect that bias.

Self-blaming and self-shaming are two of the defining mental attributes of shyness, and one of the principal ways of building the walls of the prison that is shyness. You may tell yourself that you build these walls to protect yourself from the judgments of others, but if you start to examine your thoughts, you're likely to find that you're the one doing the judging.

95

Self-judgments can be cruel and disabling, and they happen so quickly and habitually that you hardly notice them. This is like having a mean-spirited background narrator making a negative running commentary about you all the time. I've heard people refer to these nasty little internal characters as gremlins or "my mini-me," and gangs of these mean-spirited subpersonalities are sometimes labeled the "shitty committee." When you live with these kinds of thoughts, it's like always being watched by a panel of Olympic judges looking only to remove points. I've pictured my own gremlin as a mean-looking little monster with a bellows, pumping away to fan the red-hot coal of self-blame into flames. I am the one who gets consumed by this cruel burning.

As odious as the internal critic is, as mentioned in chapter 2 it's useful to find ways to recognize and acknowledge it. Identifying this mental activity can help you free yourself from its spell, and from the self-created prison of shyness. The moment you step into the position of witnessing the critic, you see from a perspective that's independent of the critic. You then have many more choices about how to look at those self-judgments and how to respond to them.

One of the dilemmas inherent in recognizing the self-destructive habit of judging is that you may find yourself judging yourself for judging yourself! When you notice judgments, it's enough to just acknowledge them and let them be. A simple internal comment like "That's a judgment" can help you free yourself from the whole judgment trap.

In their book *Embracing Ourselves* (1998), Hal and Sidra Stone remind us that critics need love too. It may seem counterintuitive and odd to relate to these mean-spirited characters this way, but it's actually a powerful way to start putting energy into something you do want as opposed to struggling with something you don't. By relating to the vicious and often unexamined habit of self-judgment consciously, you can shift from being a victim to being a compassionate witness. This alone can begin to assuage the flames of suffering and stop you from punishing yourself or imprisoning yourself in self-blame or shame. Loving-kindness and compassionate awareness may be the ultimate "get out of jail free card."

There is such a thing as exercising good judgment, but that isn't the type of judgment I'm discussing. Exercising good judgment means making decisions wisely, based on accurate information filtered through a frame of reference that's sound and true. Ironically, in order to exercise good judgment, you have to be nonjudgmental. You cultivate nonjudging by noticing when you're judging, catching yourself, forgiving yourself for judging, and then beginning again.

You can recognize when you're being self-critical and provide so much space around a nasty little commentary that it no longer seems so prominent or even important to listen to. This is something like the space that even Category 5 hurricanes eventually disappear into. In the same way that the atmosphere is infinitely more vast than hurricanes and ultimately disperses them, your awareness is infinitely more vast than your critical thoughts and ultimately can disperse even the worst of thought storms.

One of the greatest fruits of mindfulness practice is to grow in nonjudging and directly experience the world and yourself without the filter of critical interpretations. Coming to see just what is seen and hear just what is heard is liberating.

Feelings of Inadequacy

When you listen to and perform for your internal critic, you're likely to find that you can do your very best and try your hardest, but somehow never quite make it to "good enough." It can be like a nightmare where you're pursuing something you desperately need, and somehow it always remains out of reach. This is one of the traps of shyness. You may think that by doing better or being better you'll no longer feel anxious about being around other people, but since you're probably your own worst critic, this strategy doesn't work.

I call this failed strategy the "never-good-enough trap," and there's a reason why it doesn't work: You look at yourself with a critical eye, then go to work on yourself to appease or please the internal critic. The critic says, "Not good enough," and the performer tries harder. This can go on for a long time before you realize that this internal judge is never going to be satisfied, even with the best of your performances. Like all subpersonalities, this part of yourself never wants to die. Being based on pointing out what's wrong with you, it must sustain itself by always have something to comment on negatively, and it will never run out of material, because none of us will ever be perfect. It's possible to spend your entire life in the never-good-enough trap.

Habitually giving your attention to the internal critic is like frequently looking into a makeup mirror that magnifies and illuminates every flaw in your face. You can come to believe that the pores on your nose really are hideously large. Mindfulness is the antidote. It's non-judgmental and allows you to see yourself from a wide-open awareness that isn't bent on improvement. From this perspective, you can recognize when you're giving attention to the critic and being shamed into what mindfulness teacher and author Tara Brach calls the trance of unworthiness (Brach 2004). This recognition is important and provides you the opportunity to practice what she and others refer to as radical acceptance and thereby dispel this painful trance with the openhearted attention of mindfulness and self-compassion. Radical acceptance involves accepting yourself and your flaws, and even accepting the nasty little critic that claims it's just trying to help you.

Self-Criticism Projected Outward

A sense of inadequacy tends to spill over into relationships with others. As you come to think you're inadequate or inherently flawed, you're likely to imagine that others judge you in the same critical ways. Here's how this form of projection works: You have a critical thought. Since you think it, you assume it must be true. And if it is true, of course other people are going to think the same thing. As you imagine that others are thinking or saying the same cruel things about you as you say about yourself, you can end up mentally proving to yourself again and again that your self-judgments are accurate. Looking at others through this filter, you're likely to interpret things in a way that offers "proof" to reinforce your sense of shame. It's no wonder that you shy away from others.

When you feel shy, anything you do in front of other people can seem like a performance in front of an audience, even something as simple as walking in a crosswalk in front of people. You can imagine that they're judging you for how you're walking or how you look. When I was a teenager, my social anxiety was so extreme that I sometimes limped through crosswalks hoping my imagined audience would take pity on my geeky self. Part of the work of shyness involves developing such strategies to protect yourself from imagined judgments.

jumping freight trains

Many years ago while still a college student, I went on an adventure with my girlfriend, jumping freight trains to travel from California to northern Idaho. On that trip, I learned a few things about caring for my mind that have stayed with me ever since.

To sneak rides on a freight train, you can't just go to the freight yard and get into an empty car. The yard cops are constantly on the lookout and will immediately throw you out or, worse, arrest you for trespassing. You soon learn that the only way you can actually get on a train is to wait until it has left the yard and is slowly picking up speed. Then you have to run alongside the train, find what looks like an empty car, grab the bar alongside the door, and swing yourself in. Only at this point can you be sure there is no one else in the car. It's a good idea to look around as soon as you can, because some menacing-looking characters may have gotten there before you. If that's the case, you'll want to jump back out before the train picks up too much steam, because no one gets off the train after it gets up to speed.

Dealing with trains of thought is no different. If you pay attention, you can check out a thought before it picks up too much speed and you find yourself stuck with some very unpleasant thoughts for company. The trick is to recognize the nature of these thoughts early and then decide not to go along for the ride. Through mindful awareness, you can learn to recognize these thoughts for what they are. It's helpful to name them, perhaps saying something like "Oh yeah, that's my old 'I'm such a fool' thought," "I'm having that 'They don't like me' thought," or "That's a trip into the future (or into the past)." Acknowledging these thoughts in some way is a powerful way to get off the thought train or derail it altogether, freeing you from ruminations that could make you miserable for hours or even years to come.

Sometimes meditation practice involves just watching the whole train go by without getting on any of the cars, whether they are appealing or unappealing. From the position of just watching your train of thought, it can feel liberating to let it rumble on by. You'll probably notice that certain familiar freight cars appear again and again. That's because a lot of our thoughts are just a repetition of the same thoughts we had yesterday, the day before, and the day before that.

mindfulness practice:
Freight Trains of Thought

To begin this practice, please pause for five to ten minutes, or as long as you like, to practice mindful breathing.

As you continue to practice conscious breathing, let the sensation of the breath recede into the background of your awareness and remain there as a way to stay oriented in the present moment. In the foreground, notice your thoughts appear and go by. Notice that each thought has a beginning and an end. Imagine that you're sitting and watching a train go by, and that each of these thoughts is like one of the cars of the train. You aren't looking for a car to jump onto here; you're just watching them go by. You may notice that many of the freight cars of thought are remarkably similar or even identical. You may notice that some seem interesting and appealing and some seem repulsive and aversive. Let each one just go by until the train passes altogether, the dust settles, and it becomes quiet once again.

Notes to Yourself

Take some time to write about your trains of thought reflection in your journal. Did you notice any repetitive or familiar thoughts? Did you notice any that were particularly charged and compelling? Did any of your thoughts actually suck you in and take you for a ride? Were you able to choose not to get on a particular "thought car" or get off as soon as you noticed where you were? Did the train eventually pass you by, or did cars just keep coming endlessly?

noting mental states

Noting is silently acknowledging what you notice in the mind and body. It's a way to be present for what's happening now with awareness and without trying to change anything you notice. Research indicates that people who use noting to acknowledge mental states have greater mental flexibility and are more capable of regulating their emotions (Siegel 2007b). Noting mental states allows you to develop a mind-set of approaching difficult thoughts, rather than avoiding them, which would only strengthen their grip. In the moments when you're observing and acknowledging mental and emotional states, you aren't dwelling within them or being controlled by them; rather, you can just acknowledge them and let them be with openness and spaciousness of mind. This will help you develop greater equanimity and resilience. While noting mental states, you're attending to the flow of consciousness without being swept up in its contents, allowing you to witness mental states with compassion and without judgment or resistance.

mindfulness practice:
Mental Noting

To begin, practice mindful breathing in a sitting posture for ten to fifteen minutes.

As you continue to practice conscious breathing, settle into your moment-to-moment experience as an observer of the changing patterns of your physical and mental states. Note your sensations and let them be; for example, "sore knee" or "cool shoulders." Unless the sensation is extremely uncomfortable, see if you can let it be and refocus on the breath. Also note thoughts and emotions and let them be. For example, you can acknowledge any thought with the word "thinking" and let it be. Alternatively, you may choose to note something more specific about the thoughts and emotions you observe, like "planning," "worrying," or "boredom." If you choose to be more specific, keep it simple. The longer the label, the more likely you are to become caught up in it. Think of it as identifying what's happening in your mental atmosphere silently, with as few words as possible.

The intention of this practice is not to actively search for mental states, but to sit quietly and observe what arises. As you become more adept in this practice, it will become more effortless. You'll notice and acknowledge your internal experience, note it, and let it go. If nothing arises, simply be with the breath as an anchor to the present moment. During this practice, you're likely to notice that the judging mind can be quite active. There will be thoughts and feelings that you like and don't like, that you feel attracted to or repulsed by. Just acknowledge them as pleasant, unpleasant, or neutral; for example, "unpleasant thought" or "pleasant emotion." Some mental states may bring up attachment, in which case you can acknowledge "clinging." Others will bring up aversion, in which case you might acknowledge "repulsion" or "aversion." Let everything come and go as it will and let everything be.

Noting is a way to build and nourish your ability to observe without attachment or resistance. Its nature is friendly, welcoming, and compassionate toward everything that arises, even as it allows you to disidentify with the states of mind that are always coming and going. It helps you recognize that you are more the sky than you are the passing clouds and changes in the weather.

As you continue to practice noting, you'll discover that the part of you that likes and dislikes things becomes less important to you and therefore less active. Noting is a skill that gradually becomes so subtle that it requires no effort or special intention from you. You can practice noting formally or informally and make it a way of life as you come to witness mental states in everything you do. Every time you note a mental state, you step away from it a little.

Notes to Yourself

Please take a little time to write a bit about your noting practice, particularly how your mental and emotional experience changed (if it did) when you noted it. Were there some mental states that were more repetitive than others? Did some thoughts call forth emotions or physical sensations? Did some emotions call forth certain thoughts or stories? Were you able to keep your mental notes succinct and brief?

schedule practice

Please take a moment now to schedule a daily mindfulness practice with freight trains of thought and noting. It will serve you best to do one every day, perhaps alternating the two practices from day to day.

a calling to remember

Thoughts are a powerful force in shaping and coloring your world. Like a filter between you and the direct experience of this moment, thoughts interpret and define everything you see and can actually create much suffering in your life. They are central in generating anxiety, and through them you become the author of your own suffering or of your own happiness. An important message to take from this chapter is that you have a choice about whether or not to jump on trains of thought. Being present in awareness, you can watch thoughts go by and see that they are impermanent and, more importantly, are not you. You can see and understand that thoughts themselves aren't the central problem of shyness; it's how you relate to your thoughts that creates problems.

By examining your thoughts as mental events rather than reality, you can begin to dismantle some of the personal narratives that have created so much anxiety for you. You can recognize when you're scanning the future and quit falling for your mind's sometimes distorted prediction of what lies ahead.

All of your work with this book up to this point has established a foundation of mindfulness practice. You've explored the value of embracing the nonverbal world and centering yourself in the body as a way to work with thoughts that create anxiety. In the next chapter you'll learn about the power of emotions and ways you can regulate them and bring yourself more into conscious alignment with them.

welcoming 6 emotions

Your vision will become clear only when you look into your heart.
Who looks outside, dreams. Who looks inside, awakens.

—Carl Jung

In the poem "The Guest House," which appears at the beginning of part 3 of this book, twelfth-century mystic Rumi compares the human being to a guesthouse, and emotions to visitors. He advises welcoming all visitors, as "each has been sent as a guide from beyond" (1995, p. 109). However, an important point to note is that a guesthouse is for *guests*, who are by definition temporary visitors. Emotions are indeed like that: impermanent, very short-term visitors. A mood might be an overnight guest, but emotions, like thoughts, can come and go in seconds—unless you get caught up in entertaining them or struggling with them. In this chapter, you'll explore how to cultivate clarity and *equanimity*, or composure, so that you can welcome emotions without being overwhelmed by them.

the nature of emotions

Much can be learned from these momentary visitors if you can invite them in and listen to them. On the other hand, if you avoid and hide your emotions, you can't learn to respond to them in a healthy way and will deny yourself the benefits they can bring. Furthermore, blocked emotions don't just disappear. They accumulate and even grow, and can ultimately overwhelm and undermine you.

A big part of how each of us relates to emotions is learned very early in life. By age four or five we've learned to welcome and entertain certain emotions, such as fear, sorrow, and anger, or have become avoidant of the emotions we don't want to feel. We learn these things in relationship with our primary caregivers. Sometimes children are admonished, "Stop crying or I'll give you something to cry about." Sometimes when they're afraid, their fears are laughed at, they're told not to feel afraid, and they may even be forced into the very things that scare them. Even happiness and laughter can be treated as too much. I remember walking by the front of a neighbor's house years ago and hearing a mother yelling out the kitchen window, "Quit laughing so loud! Don't you know how hard I'm working in here!" In our homes, schools, and churches, we are too often taught that our emotions are unwelcome and to close the door to them.

As our emotions are shaped and conditioned so early in life, they are deeply ingrained in our personalities and happen automatically. They arise in reaction to certain mental and environmental cues with such amazing rapidity that we can't even witness the evaluative process that triggers them (Goleman 2003). Science has come to recognize emotions as an integral element of our interpersonal neurobiology; they help us navigate the complex terrain of interpersonal relationships. Our emotions tell us to draw closer to or pull away from others, to create boundaries or alliances, or to speak up or shut up. From the scientific perspective, our emotions are vitally important, helping us cooperate with one another in a spirit of mutual support that has been, and remains, essential to our survival as a species.

One of life's great challenges is learning to self-regulate your emotions—in other words, learning to listen to and honor your emotions without being taken over by them. If you can't feel your emotions and maintain enough balance to act responsibly from them, you won't know how to proceed through the many perilous twists and turns of your interactions with others.

Paul Ekman, Ph.D., reports from the enormous body of research he's conducted on emotions that there are up to ten basic emotions: anger, fear, sadness, disgust, contempt, surprise, enjoyment, embarrassment, guilt, and shame, each representing a family of emotions. For example, the fear family includes anxiety, terror, apprehension, worry, and so on, and has its origins in negative expectations (Goleman 2003; Ekman and Davidson 1995).

responding to emotions

That we have emotions is a given. How we react or respond to them is a matter of choice. As discussed in chapter 3, Victor Frankl offered the important insight that there's a space between stimulus and response, and if we can pause and bring the full light of our awareness into that space, we can free ourselves from automatic reactions that are often dysfunctional. Mindfulness practice will allow you to recognize that space and use it to respond to your emotions with clarity, compassion, and skillfulness.

It's likely that your reactions to difficult emotions create much of the suffering you experience in regard to shyness and social anxiety. On one hand, the more you try to block, avoid, control, or escape difficult emotions, the more certain they are to revisit you time and time again and become problematic. On the other hand, if you're swept up by each passing emotion, you'll find yourself careening from one overwhelming event to the next. But if you can learn to attend to difficult emotions with clear awareness and acceptance, you may be able to find a middle ground where you can work with your emotional states more skillfully. The intention is to be with difficult emotions without inflaming them or being driven by them. When you begin accepting and conversing with your difficult emotions, you'll find that they have much to teach you about who you are and how you can more effectively navigate your most difficult and complex interpersonal relationships.

working with emotions

Up to this point, you've invested a lot of time in developing skills that will help you undertake the important work of transforming your relationship with difficult emotions like anxiety. For example, the skills and perspectives you've developed in working with thoughts will also be helpful with emotions, in part because of how thoroughly intertwined thoughts and emotions are. As with thoughts, you can turn toward difficult emotions by feeling into them, acknowledging them, and letting them be. Anxiety itself may become an object of compassionate investigation when you find a place within yourself to witness it without pushing it away or being overwhelmed by it.

When you turn inward to mindfully witness your own inner process, you'll notice that you become aware of emotions only after they begin. However, you may be able to see that a thought or environmental cue immediately preceded that emotion. You'll also notice that until you began working on mindfulness of your inner state, the interplay of your thoughts and emotions generally happened outside your conscious awareness.

Like thoughts, emotions play a large part in shaping and coloring your interpretations and perceptions of the world. Let's look at how thoughts and emotions are intertwined using an example from earlier, about giving a presentation in front of a group of people. If you identify as shy, this probably makes you feel frightened, and this emotion could lead to the thought that the audience is judging you harshly. You might then look around the room to discover a lot of frowning faces, which you interpret as confirmation of what you expected to be true. The curious thing about this perception is that someone in a comfortable and secure state of mind who happens to think he or she is a fabulous speaker could look around the same room, see only smiling and nodding faces, and go away believing that everyone loved the presentation. Recall the quotation from the Talmud at the beginning of chapter 5, which expresses that we see things as we are, not as things themselves are. Our perceptions generally conform to our expectations.

The many ways that emotions and thoughts play off of one another to color your perceptions can become the object of mindfulness as you witness what you feel and hold it in awareness. It's challenging to stay with and investigate difficult emotions—to stay present with fear and anxiety long enough to recognize how difficult thoughts and emotions are playing into your perceptions and actions. Just looking at emotions in this way begins to create some space between fear and the urge to escape or avoid interactions. Each time you turn toward fear from this place of self-observation, you can increase that space and free yourself a little more from the old habits that comprise your shyness pattern. Each time you welcome and entertain these difficult guests, you can diminish both the intensity of the fear and the amount of time it takes you to recover your equanimity.

This work is difficult, but it's worthwhile, as it will allow you to disengage the automatic connections between your thoughts and emotions and short-circuit the self-propagating feedback loop that ties you in knots when you're around other people. It's liberating to learn to live with rather than from your emotions.

living a short distance away from your body

It isn't unusual for people who feel shy to live mostly in a mental world dominated by thoughts tinged with anxiety. In his short story "A Painful Case," James Joyce created a character named Mr. Duffy, who lived "at a little distance from his body, regarding his own acts with doubtful side-glasses" (2006, 86), making up stories about himself in the third person and the past tense as he went about his day. Anyone who feels shy can relate to Mr. Duffy, because this is exactly how it feels to live with social anxiety. If you feel anxious around and with other people, it's not unusual to imagine yourself some short distance from your body, looking at yourself critically as a performer who's supposed to have some specified, correct appearance and behavior. Perhaps a large amount of shyness can be characterized as avoiding emotions and looking at oneself critically from that imaginary vantage point: "He was too anxious. He was too frightened. He didn't talk right, didn't walk right, and didn't even smile right. He can't get anything right when he's with a group of people."

The truth is, no one ever gets anything right from this perspective. As long as you're looking at yourself from somewhere outside yourself and trying to perform to what you believe to be the standards of others, you will be judging and striving. You'll be trapped in doing mode and out of touch with your more authentic, whole self. It's not our emotions that cause so much pain and suffering—it's how we relate to them. It's how we close the door on our feelings and then question and doubt our behavior and try to look "right," whatever that is. In fact, if you befriend your emotions and quit making them into something that's being judged by an imaginary, critical audience, you'll be better able to regulate them, and better able to respond to challenging social situations, rather than reacting to them.

the body as friend and ally

The body is a place where you can become more grounded and stable in working with difficult emotions like anxiety and fear. It can be an important ally in meeting challenging emotions and dealing with them well. As with physical pain, we need emotional pain to navigate in this world—sometimes quite literally. For example, there's a very real value in the fear you experience when someone is driving recklessly near you. It's immediate, and your fear can help you be more alert and adept at steering clear of that driver. Similarly, anxiety that comes up before an important life event can help you better prepare for that event. The key is learning to respond to anxiety with clarity and skill rather than denial and shame.

To know who you are and live fully into all that you may be requires that you feel your emotions—all of them, not just the ones that feel good and that you like and want. In fact, the emotions that you don't want to feel often hold the greatest potential for healing and liberation. Centering your awareness in your body will give you a place to ground and keep your balance while facing your fear.

Here's an example: When you converse with an attractive friend at work, your heart starts pounding in your chest and you feel that familiar urge to make fear the center of your attention and react by fleeing. This time, however, you try something different. You don't make an excuse and escape. You turn toward the fear and acknowledge it. You shift your attention into the sensations you feel in that moment and use them to return to the here and now. Grounded in your body and in the moment, you can witness the internal cascade of thoughts and emotions. You can acknowledge fear and let it be, then bring your attention back to your friend. As you invest all of your attention into listening to and empathizing with this person, fear arises again and tugs at you, this time churning in the pit of your stomach. You turn toward your belly with kindness and compassion as you might turn toward and comfort a frightened child. Then you let your belly be and bring your attention back into the conversation.

It's not easy, but gradually you can begin turning toward your fear with more tenderness, kindness, and acceptance—and recognition that the fear doesn't really have anything to do with the person or what you're talking about. Fear is just fear. It's nothing more than an unpleasant emotion. Bear in mind that emotions can't hurt you, but how you

109

react to them certainly can. For example, fear can hurt you in this situation if you let it capture you in a private self-consciousness where you're consumed with it and trying to hide it. You'll suffer, the interaction will suffer, and your relationship with the person will suffer.

turning toward emotion

Turning toward emotion via sensations in the body is a brief but kind visit to yourself—a temporary shift of attention to care for and calm yourself so that you can return to the situation with greater presence and awareness. It gives you a chance to look for places where you can extend compassion to yourself. You may also notice that when you're no longer focused on escape and avoidance, you can feel a growing sense of compassion and generosity of spirit with others.

Anxiety is an intense emotion, and one of the most challenging to work with. When it arises in your meditation practice, just the intention to acknowledge it and let it be will help, because that approach is so dramatically different than typical responses of suppressing or being possessed by anxiety. As you sit with it, you'll also notice all of your old strategies to avoid it, which can also be very helpful. For example, noticing the way the body contracts somewhere as you feel an impulse to avoid an emotion or thought gives you an indicator to detect when you're responding similarly in day-to-day circumstances. In this way, recognizing emotions and related physical sensations in meditation practice is directly transferable into your day-to-day life, allowing you to pause and bring awareness and compassion into emotional reactions as they come up in social situations. To be clear, you aren't employing awareness to change what you feel, but rather to witness and learn to better respond to what you feel.

Still, sometimes fear and anxiety can be too large to approach or be with, particularly when they're related to trauma. In such cases, the wisest and most compassionate response may be to use a prescription medication to reduce the anxiety enough that you can begin to approach and work with it. If you feel like medication could be right for you, consult a physician or psychologist. And if you do choose to use medications, realize that with time and practice, emotion-regulation skills may eventually be all you need to manage fear or anxiety, allowing you to reduce or even stop taking anxiety medications.

pain education

Pain can be a great teacher, but it's a class few of us care to attend. I learned one of my first important lessons about physical pain as a teen, from a welder at a muffler shop. He told me that it was important for him to feel the back pain he suffered: "The doctors told me that if I didn't feel this pain, I could hurt my back so badly I may never work again. If I listen to it, I'll know how I can safely move." It had never occurred to me that pain in any shape could be a good thing.

Pain in all its forms can play a role in health and growth, providing education that we might not always welcome, but that can generally be beneficial. The word "educate" is derived from the Latin word *educare*, which means "to lead out or draw forth." As you turn toward pain with awareness, it may draw forth a torrent of tears—and with them a disowned part of yourself that longs to be known and reunited into your personality. Sometimes you just need to soften your resistance and let pain lead you to discoveries you can't anticipate. In meditation practice it's possible to become more skillful in working with and honoring painful thoughts and feelings, just as that welder became more sensitive and responsive to his physical pain.

Feeling into pain of all sorts, physical, mental, or emotional, with openhearted awareness isn't easy, and this skill won't grow unless you practice it with patience and perseverance. But it's a valuable ability that will enable you to work more skillfully with difficult emotions like fear and anxiety. It will help you accept what you need to accept and let go of what you need to let go of, including efforts to avoid and escape the social world, which you can never completely escape anyway. Pain can be just pain—an unpleasant sensation. Fear can be just fear—an unpleasant emotion. Not all teachers are pleasant.

• Discoveries on the Path: *Bob's Story*

Bob never seemed to do anything right. For example, talking with his boss about a new contract, he suddenly couldn't remember the name of the big company they were doing business with. His boss quickly filled in the missing name, but Bob thought he saw him rolling his eyes as they parted. "Augh!" he thought. "I can't believe I did that! Now he thinks I'm an idiot. This is the biggest opportunity I've ever been given, and

111

I've already blown it." The more angry he became, the more anxious he felt about the possibility of being replaced.

Back when Bob was in seventh grade, his father was concerned that he was far too anxious around other people and cried too often about "little" things. His parents decided he needed to join the school football team, and his father even showed up from time to time to watch him practice and talk with the coach. The coach and his team members were hard on him, calling him a sissy, a girl, a crybaby. Nearly every practice was an ordeal of hurt feelings and humiliation. Why were they doing this to him? He hadn't done anything to hurt them. He hated the whole thing and eventually quit, earning his father's contempt.

But the experience deeply affected Bob. He didn't feel as safe anymore, or as open. Ultimately he did learn a lesson: Don't show anyone your emotions. Don't trust anyone. He came to hate his anxious feelings, and in time this set of emotions and reactions developed into the social anxiety that was threatening his career. Bob read about the benefits of mindfulness with anxiety in a magazine and came to my mindfulness-based psychotherapy practice looking for instruction in meditation and help with social anxiety.

Bob's pathway into mindfulness involved entering into and feeling a lot of unpleasant emotions that he'd bottled up for years. A deep hurt and loneliness emerged from his inquiries into fear and anxiety, and he also found a trembling anger that he'd tried to squelch his entire life. As he brought more light into the dark places of his disowned emotions, he learned more about his social anxiety. One day he told me, "I refuse to be like my father! I will never, ever hurt or scare anyone like he did. I hated his anger, and I hate my own anger." We talked a lot about his anger and he gradually realized that hating and not wanting his anger didn't make it disappear and may even have intensified it. He developed an intention to acknowledge his anger and look for ways to express it that fit with his highest values—to see if there was a way for him to be angry without acting from it in ways that injured anyone.

In just a few weeks of living with this intention, Bob realized that his efforts to never say or do anything to hurt anyone hadn't included treating himself with the same compassion and care. As we talked one day, he realized he had now come full circle, and he recalled how self-critical and angry at himself he'd been when talking with his boss several months before. Under his meek and mild-mannered exterior, he had discovered an inner critic at the core of his anxiety that fed off all the anger, hurt, and frustration he tried to avoid.

In the months that followed, Bob joined a weekly meditation group and made many more discoveries about his lifelong habit of swallowing anger and feeling self-critical, and he began to see how this led to his social anxiety. At our last meeting, he realized just how much progress he'd made, as he recalled a recent incident in which he once again stuck his foot in his mouth, but this time he didn't beat himself up over it and even made a joke about it. He knew he still had much to learn about managing emotions in a healthy way, but now he knew what direction he needed to go.

Working with anxiety of all kinds involves a willingness to turn toward and be with emotions that you may have spent much of your life trying to avoid. Bob discovered that he had been denying and swallowing anger for many years and learned that when he could hold the anger in awareness and acceptance, his experience of anxiety changed. The invitation is to approach powerful and long dispossessed emotions gradually, with curiosity and patience. Know that you can take your time and find your own way to integrate difficult emotions that's balanced and right for you.

Finding that balance can be a lot like learning downhill skiing. There's a critical moment where you have to lean into a place that's considerably forward of what seems safe and comfortable in order to stay upright and balanced as you hurtle down a mountain. As it turns out, holding yourself back in what feels like the comfort zone will actually cause tumble after tumble. Once you find this point of balance, you discover a *new* comfort zone where you have a sense of control and mastery of what previously seemed like a headlong freefall.

You stand in a similar place now in regard to working with difficult emotions. Although it's challenging and may seem counterintuitive, the best way to explore the terrain of anxiety and fear is to leave your comfort zone and lean into the emotions.

mindfulness practice:
Mindful Yoga

Mindful yoga is a powerful practice for becoming more sensitive to the body and its signals, and for learning to tolerate distress. Not only does yoga help you ground your awareness in the body and in the present moment, it also offers you a way to feel how the mind and body are connected and how emotions are expressed in the sensations you feel. With yoga, you can learn to be with and investigate uncomfortable and sometimes even painful physical sensations. This can inform the process of learning how to be with and investigate unpleasant emotions.

In yoga practice, you bring yourself into a posture and remain at the edge of a stretch without trying to force yourself to stretch any farther; rather, you stay near that painful edge and wait, sensitively and patiently, for a release. Sometimes you may even back off a little so you can continue to breathe freely near the edge. As you wait and breathe into the pain, you're feeling right into the holding and tightness with a soft and accepting curiosity. You wait until you feel something open and give a little, and then you find that you can settle a little more deeply into the posture. You've discovered, rather than forced, a release. In yoga, you're physically present without striving or trying to force progress and, most importantly, without resisting or trying to escape from your experience, even when it's a little painful to you. This will later prove to be an excellent model for working with difficult emotions.

A good time to do this yoga practice is before you meditate in the morning, as a way to care for your body and get the kinks out after a night's sleep. As in our other practices, it would be helpful for you to record this practice for yourself or to purchase these practices from www.mindfullivingprograms.com.

1. Begin by lying on a blanket or mat on the floor, or on a carpeted floor. Lie on your back with your legs stretched out and your arms at your sides. Notice where your body is making contact with the floor, and feel into the sensations of being supported by the earth beneath you. Be aware of your bodily sensations. Breathing in and breathing out, settle into this place.

2. Welcome yourself to this place and offer yourself some gratitude for taking this time to be with yourself with awareness and compassion. Know that you are giving yourself a gift that will help you learn how to honor your body and its limits, just as you are learning to honor your emotions and their limits, without pushing yourself to go beyond what feels right for you.

3. Notice your breath coming and going and, as best as possible, stay in touch with your in breath and out breath throughout the following movements and gentle stretches.

4. As you inhale, bring the right knee up to the chest and, if you can, reach down with your hands to grasp your leg, either immediately beneath the kneecap or at the back of the thigh, right behind the knee. Without pulling or forcing the knee into your chest, see if you can relax into this posture, feeling the places in your body that are experiencing some stretch or sensation.

5. Breathing in and out normally and naturally, see if you can direct your breath into the tight places a little more each time you exhale. If you notice your breath has become labored or has moved up into your chest, release the stretch a little and see if the breath can flow easily from the belly. Resting here and feeling into the places in your body where there's tension or pain, and waiting for a sensation of release. Notice what's happening in the rest of your body as you breathe in and out. Has your neck contracted in any way? If it has, see if you might release the tension by bringing your chin a little closer to your chest. Stay in this posture for a minute or so, extending the stretch a little if you want, and notice whether any of the places in your body that are tense and holding release a little.

6. When you're ready, slowly and mindfully let your knee open once again and, as you exhale, extend your leg straight up over your body, grasping the back of the leg for support. Don't pull the leg toward your chest; let it extend to the place where it feels most comfortable. Then very slowly

turn your ankle in little circles to the right, and then to the left.

7. When you're ready, bend your knee and lower your leg to the floor again. As it touches, inhale and draw the other knee to your chest. Repeat this sequence with the left leg, being present in your body and in touch with your breath.

8. Rest for a breath or two to see how both legs feel after these stretches. Now, with an in breath, gently bring both knees to your chest and hold them in whatever way feels right for you. Breathing in and out, wait for the release.

9. Holding the back of the legs with your hands, extend both of your legs above you, gently drawing them toward your chest, to the edge of discomfort and breathing into the places that call out for attention. Being present.

10. Bend the legs and bring the feet back onto the floor near the buttocks, with the knees up and legs together. Rock the knees gently from side to side, going a little farther to the right and left with each exhalation, and then allowing the knees to fall to one side as far as they will, keeping your shoulders on the floor. Turn your head in the direction opposite the knees and relax completely into the spinal twist. When you're ready, bring the knees up with an in breath, and with the next out breath allow them to fall to the other side, again turning your head in the opposite direction to extend the twist.

11. Bring the knees upright again with an inhalation. Draw the feet a little closer to the buttocks. As you breathe out, allow the knees to separate and fall slowly out to each side, a little farther with each exhalation, until they rest at their fullest extension. Rest here for a few breaths, feeling into the tight places long enough to see if the stretch will open a bit on its own before bringing the knees back up and extending the legs out to rest on the floor.

12. Take a breath in and reach toward the ceiling with your right arm. Making little circles with your wrist as you breathe in and out, see if you might extend the stretch a

little with each out breath. When you like, allow that arm to float slowly down back over your head and rest on the floor so that it's stretching out above your head with your biceps as close to your ear as feels right to you. Breathing in and out, see how it feels to extend your arm and hand as far as you like while at the same time stretching downward with your right leg and through the heel. Feel the stretch along the right side of your body.

13. When you're ready, repeat this sequence with your left arm and leg.

14. Come back into your beginning position with both legs outstretched and your arms by your sides. Let your awareness fill your whole body as you rest in this posture at least five minutes. Notice how you can feel the breath moving in your body more fully and completely. Thank yourself for this gift of mindful yoga.

As you practice mindful yoga, you'll find many opportunities to explore areas of discomfort and grow in self-compassion with each gentle inquiry into a painful place. Your sensitive attention to your body in these moments of discomfort will make more vivid any automatic and unconscious habits of avoiding aversive physical experience. You might notice that these same escape habits come up for you with difficult emotions. The skills you develop during yoga practice for staying present and softening around physical pain will enable you to stay present and soften around emotional pain too.

Notes to Yourself

Take some time to write in your journal about what you experienced during your mindful yoga practice. Take note of the ways that you worked with tight or even painful places. Could you get near the discomfort with awareness and curiosity? Did you see how you could back off a little when the feelings were too intense and soften the tension by practicing acceptance? Did you notice any stories or emotions in relation to the tight and uncomfortable places?

calming the fear body

Mindfulness meditation can be described as creating a space in your mind in which you can witness thoughts and emotions enter and leave. Letting them come and go, you see that some are pleasant, some are neutral, and some are unpleasant, but they are all impermanent. If you can bring the same kind of awareness and mindful inquiry to emotions as you've brought to thoughts and physical sensations, you may find that even emotions as difficult as fear and anxiety are more manageable. With practice, you can begin to distinguish between primary and secondary, or reactionary, emotions. Sometimes you may become so swept up in a secondary emotion that you lose track of or even remain unconscious of what set it off. For example, let's say your boss calls you to her office and asks you to make a presentation to the entire office staff and a huge wave of anxiety sweeps over you. You agree to the assignment, but as you walk back to your desk, you become angry at yourself for feeling so anxious. The anger is a secondary emotion. Your internal dialogue about being angry can then evoke more secondary emotions that fill the rest of your day as anger gives rise to guilt, guilt gives rise to a feeling of helplessness, and then you feel another surge of anxiety.

The way out of this cascade is at the beginning—in how you respond to your initial emotion. By attending to the surge of anxiety with kind awareness rather than self-judgment and anger, you can sidetrack the uproar of secondary emotions. This way of being with difficult emotions won't come overnight, but it can grow over time.

Let's look at how that same example would unfold if you were to take this new stance: Your boss gives you this assignment and a big anxiety arises in you. You acknowledge or note "anxiety," give it some space, and feel into it with gentle curiosity. You stay. You breathe. You let the feeling of anxiety just be there. You acknowledge your anxiety with acceptance: "Ah, my old companion anxiety." As you return to your desk, a thought arises: "Who wouldn't feel anxious in the face of what I've just been asked to do?" You remind yourself that you do know a lot about what your boss has asked you to talk about, and though you don't *want* to give a presentation, you know you can do it. You breathe and stay connected to the belly as you create an outline for your talk, and in a little while you notice that you aren't feeling so anxious.

You can facilitate the body's relaxation response by just inhabiting your body with more kindness and awareness in those moments when you notice your heart beating faster with anxiety. Right in that moment, you might gently place your hand over your heart and say to yourself, "I care for this frightened heart." Then, with compassion and acceptance, spend a few minutes just being with yourself physically rather than reacting automatically with old habits and stories of self-judgment. This is a shift from self-blame to compassionate presence, from avoidance to acceptance. From this place, centered in your body and the present moment, you may also challenge the thoughts that are creating such an emotional uproar and inquire to see if they're absolutely true and whether it's necessary to heed them or even believe them. By looking at your thoughts in this way and disidentifying from them, you can then calm down a little and begin to move forward with more clarity and equanimity.

Turning to be with your anxiety with friendly attention and kind acceptance is a radical shift from the self-critical and resistance-based reactivity of the fear body. As you are being with and letting be, you are no longer feeding the fear body with more fear, and therefore no longer falling for the mind's urgent and compelling habits of escape and avoidance. Rather than being anxious and quick to escape, you can begin to acknowledge and face what's before you.

Employing a little of the knowledge about the biology of fear you learned in chapter 1 can be helpful in those moments when the fear body is activated; you can use some of the body's cues to make a shift into awareness and activate the body's self-calming system. For example, you can remember that your racing heart and rapid breathing play a vital and important role in your body's self-protection system, which is just trying to help keep you safe. Rather than viewing these physical reactions as some kind of enemy, you can recognize that this is your body's effort to help you in some way.

When you shift your awareness into a physical place grounded in the body and attend to what's happening right now, your attention can stop contracting around some idea of a future calamity and expand to take in the whole spectrum of sensations, emotions, and thoughts occurring right now. Notice the changing and impermanent nature of each of these mental and physical events and allow your attention to settle in the physical sensations. You might acknowledge that this is just another anxiety event, and that it too will pass.

By inviting compassionate awareness into an anxiety reaction, you can come to see the cascade of mental and physical reactions as separate events that are no longer fused together in a confusing and upsetting mass. Be aware that in most cases, once a strong reaction has happened, it can take fifteen or twenty minutes for the body to physically assimilate all of the self-calming hormones and chemicals it has produced and once again find its steady state. So even though the self-calming relaxation response has begun, the heart may continue to beat more rapidly for a while. Be patient with yourself; you're finding a new way to navigate in fear's waters.

White-Water Kayaking

I've learned a little about how to work with the rush of powerful feelings by kayaking in roaring white water. An important skill in kayaking is to stop periodically to study the route you're about to take in a river before you launch into it. You pull out of the rush of the river to sit a little and look for the ways you might navigate the next stretch. And before you paddle back into the river's current, you look for the next place where you can stop to rest and regroup. Interestingly, some of the best places to stop in a white-water river are directly downstream from the biggest and most menacing rocks. If you can get past these very scary places, they often provide a spot where you can rest.

As you pass one of these rocks, you drive your paddle forcefully into the water to swing your kayak right behind the rock, with the front tip of your boat resting on the back of the rock. This still place within the current is an eddy, so pulling up to stop in these still places is called eddying out. The river's current will actually hold you there, and you can sit for as long as you like to breathe and check out how you can navigate the river to the next place to eddy out.

Working with fear is much the same. You have to actually enter fear's waters to learn to navigate them. Once in the river of fear and other difficult emotions, you only need to figure out how to navigate the stretch immediately in front of you. You don't have to know how to navigate the whole river; you only need to go from rock to rock. Take comfort in knowing there are places of stillness even in the midst of the racing, chaotic currents of anxiety and fear. In the midst of an emotional uproar, shifting your attention to the here-and-now immediacy of physical sensations, even unpleasant sensations, provides a place to eddy out so you can rest and find your way.

mindfulness practice:
Releasing Fear Meditation

As you saw in yoga, you can be physically present without trying to force progress and, more importantly, without resisting or trying to escape from your experience, even when it's a little painful to you. You can work with the tight edges of fear and anxiety just as you've worked with tight muscles and joints in yoga. You can gently investigate the tense and contracted places in your mind and wait for them to release, just like you explored the contracted places in your body and waited for them to release.

This guided meditation is to assist you in releasing the tight and contracted places of fear and anxiety. In this practice you'll learn how to create a space where you can sit with fear and investigate it with a gentle and kind curiosity. Being sensitive and mindful of your well-being, know that there are some fears that are so great, such as those due to trauma, that it's best to do this practice with the assistance of a therapist or skillful and trusted friend or teacher.

1. Give yourself at least thirty minutes for this practice. Begin by choosing a place that's safe and comfortable and where you can sit without being disturbed. If you like, gather a few objects that are important to you, that you treasure, or that bring you comfort and set them nearby.

2. With your eyes slightly open and gazing softly at the floor or wall in front of you, practice mindful breathing for at least ten minutes, or as long as you like. See if you can find little releases of tension in your body each time you exhale. Notice the spaces between the breaths, particularly at the end of each exhalation, as you wait for your body to breathe in again. Let your breath come and go as it will and use the sensation of your breath to be present.

3. Bring to mind an upcoming event that elicits anxiety. Consider what it is about this situation that you find most disturbing. Notice what happens in your body, with your

breath, your belly, and your heart, as you reflect on this situation. Notice the difference between the thoughts about the situation and the sensations you feel as you consider it, and focus your attention primarily on the sensations.

4. Feel into your body. See if you can find what seems to be the strongest sensation that's arising and attend to it as closely and tenderly as possible. Bring your curiosity and compassion to this place and sit with it. Just like you might rest at the edge of a yoga stretch and breathe into the place of discomfort, sit with this unpleasant sensation and breathe into it. Notice if the anxiety changes in any way. Don't try to push through it or escape from it, just be with it with as much kindness and acceptance as possible. Notice if another story or emotion arises that becomes more prominent. Acknowledge it, let it be, and direct your attention primarily to any changes you notice in physical sensations. Notice that as you attend to the immediacy of sensations, they are in the foreground of your consciousness, and thoughts, emotions, and personal narratives are in the background. Being present in the sensations.

5. Know that you have a deep being and wholeness within you that is larger than the small and contracted self that tightens around this anxiety. You can make your wholeness your base and deep center as you simply sit with anxiety. Notice the changing nature of your sensations. See if you can physically feel when you become involved in the stories and thoughts that come up or any resistance that comes up. Notice what it feels like to return your primary attention to physical sensations. Every time you find yourself identified with stories, thoughts, and emotions, acknowledge them, let them be, and return to sensations. If you do nothing but this for this entire practice, it will be time well spent.

6. You may notice that different sensations seem to release, just like the body releases at the edge in a yoga posture. You may notice many different thoughts and emotions are a part of anxiety and fear, and that they come and go: a disturbing thought; a moment of anxiety; a moment of contraction; a moment of resistance; a moment of surrender.

Each thought and emotion coming and going, just like breaths come and go. Letting yourself soften around the hard sensations, wait for a release into greater spaciousness. See if you can stay with this practice until you feel a release in the area of the most intense sensation. By letting yourself be with yourself with compassion, you can discover that there is a vastness within you that is large enough to contain this anxiety and expand around it.

7. You may acknowledge to yourself, "I'm feeling anxious right now, but I'm okay. It's just unpleasant and it won't last forever." If you want, and if it's helpful, you can shift your attention from the places of greatest discomfort in your body to another place or sensation in your body that's less intense. Use this place to eddy out, catch your breath, and rest until you're ready to forge back into the white water of intense sensations. Eddy out whenever you like. Begin again whenever you like. Be with yourself with compassion and loving-kindness. Each moment of sensation and fear is another chance to embrace yourself with awareness and tenderness.

8. When you're ready to bring this practice to a close, return to mindfulness of breathing. As thoughts and emotions come up, acknowledge them, let them be, and bring your attention back into your breath.

9. As you conclude this practice, congratulate yourself for reaching for the strength and courage to face your fears and thank yourself for giving yourself this gift of mindfulness and loving-kindness.

Notes to Yourself

Take a few minutes to write in your journal about what you experienced during this practice. Please take special note of anything you discovered you could do with moments of fear or anxiety other than trying to control or escape from them.

Exercise:
Exploring Your Unpleasant Emotions

Just as with kayaking a white-water river, it's important to know as much as you can about your most challenging emotions before you launch into working with them directly. You can do this by creating a list of unpleasant emotions you experience over the next week. Please record your unpleasant emotions for at least a few days before reading on, as you'll use events from the list in the next exercise.

First, record the emotion itself, then record the event that caused it, keeping in mind that an event can be external, such as a social situation, or internal, such as a thought about some past or future situation. Use as few words as possible to note the event that triggered the emotion, then record the sensations you experienced as a result, and the ways you reacted, such as avoiding, escaping, rationalizing, and so on. Use the form below as a template for recording your unpleasant emotions in your shyness journal. (For a downloadable version of this form to print out, see my website, www.mindfullivingprograms.com.)

unpleasant emotions				
	Emotion	Event	Sensations	Reactions
Monday				
Tuesday				
Wednesday				
Thursday				
Friday				
Saturday				
Sunday				

Exercise:
Caring for Unpleasant Emotions

You can face and work with any unpleasant emotion, like fear, shame, or grief, using the "Releasing Fear Meditation" from earlier in this chapter. Drawing from your list of unpleasant emotions, give yourself at least thirty minutes for the following exercise.

1. Choose the least challenging emotion and event from your list of unpleasant emotions to work with first.

2. Use the "Releasing Fear Meditation" to feel into that emotion and work with it. If possible, stay with the emotion until it decreases in intensity a little, then eddy out in your breath and body.

3. After a rest, return to the emotion again and again, as many times as necessary, until the emotion no longer has the same charge or intensity when you return to it.

4. If you're up for it, go ahead and choose a more challenging emotion and begin to work with it. Alternatively, you can take up a more challenging emotion the next time you're ready to do this practice.

5. In the days and weeks to come, continue working on the emotions on your list, from least to most challenging, in the same way. At the end of each practice, congratulate and thank yourself for your efforts, regardless of the outcome.

Stinging Nettle Wisdom

If you've ever brushed up against a stinging nettle plant, you quickly discovered how it got its name: Almost as soon as you touch it, your skin turns red and stings like the blazes! Amazingly, there's something you can do to get immediate relief—and it's drawn from the very thing that just hurt you. Using a glove or wrapping your hand to protect it, pull up the plant that just stung you (not an act of revenge, honest!). Hold the plant by the root and cut the stem in two with a crosswise cut, being careful of the fine hairs that line its stem and leaves, because they cause the stinging. Let the stinging nettle juice drip onto your burning flesh. You'll get immediate relief. The stinging nettle's juice is the antidote to its own sting.

Likewise, the healing balm of anxious and scary feelings can be found in the emotions themselves. This is why mindful awareness is so beneficial with shyness and social anxiety: It allows you to be with and deeply investigate the things that scare you in a way that soothes their sting.

schedule practice

Please take a moment now to schedule daily mindfulness practice with mindful yoga and another mindfulness practice, preferably a stillness practice like the body scan. It will serve you best to practice every day, perhaps alternating the two practices from day to day. You can practice the "Releasing Fear Meditation" anytime you feel anxious.

a calling to remember

With mindfulness and compassion, you can learn to welcome and befriend your emotions even when they're extremely unpleasant. View them as temporary guests, meeting them at the door and welcoming them into your consciousness. Listen to see if you can learn anything from these visitors. This is one of the keys to freeing yourself from the pain of shyness and social anxiety. In this chapter, you've opened the door to emotions to better understand the role they play in your life. To learn from your emotions, you must find ways to enter them, know them, and honor them as a part of you.

In the next chapter, we'll invest in mindfulness practices that can help you work with difficult emotions with more acceptance and self-compassion. You'll study your patterns of social aversion, learn how aversion keeps you stuck in your anxiety and shyness, and then learn how to get unstuck. A big part of this work is honoring your hurt and frightened feelings and extending loving-kindness and compassion toward these places in yourself.

the wisdom of turning toward

7

Security is mostly a superstition. It does not exist in nature, nor do the children of men as a whole experience it. Avoiding danger is no safer in the long run than outright exposure. Life is either a daring adventure, or nothing. To keep our faces toward change and behave like free spirits in the presence of fate is strength undefeatable.

—Helen Keller

When you look deeply into stress-related symptoms, you can sometimes find clues about their origins in what a person is trying to avoid. A woman who has swallowed her angry words develops a jaw or throat problem, or a man who has hardened his heart toward his children because they supported his wife in a bitter divorce develops heart problems. Anxiety is often the expression of emotions we don't want to feel, like shame, anger, or hatred. When we're unwilling or unable to come to terms with these emotions, they fuel much of the anxiety in our lives. Psychologists call this *pathogenesis*, a word that literally means "to generate suffering," and *experiential avoidance* because it's an attempt to avoid unpleasant experiences.

Some avoidance skills are essential, as when you try to put more distance between yourself and an erratic driver, but many avoidance patterns are unconscious and cause more injury than benefit. Because unconscious and automatic avoidance patterns are a primary cause of the suffering in shyness and social anxiety, this chapter will give you tools to better respond to the things you block and avoid.

getting stuck

There are endless ways to avoid the things you don't want to think or feel or do. You can block, resist, control, or escape them with drugs, alcohol, work, shopping, or adventures in virtual reality. You can hide out in your TV, in your bed, in your computer, or in fantasies in your head. But all attempts at avoidance ultimately lead to the same fate. These efforts just get you more stuck in whatever you're trying to escape. Even avoiding scary dogs can leave you with an intractable fear of dogs. The more you avoid things, the less chance you get to test the reality of your fears, and the scarier things seem.

As your mindful awareness grows, you can begin to notice the ways you suppress or skip over certain thoughts and emotions that you don't want or don't like. You're also likely to notice how the thoughts you don't want are the very ones that tend to come around again and again, getting you more stuck in the effort to avoid them. This is one of the great values of mindfulness meditation: It provides a means of investigating the ways you seek to escape from things that are unpleasant.

For many people, the most vexatious avoidance trap is the fear of experiencing the discomfort of negative emotions. You can end up expending a great deal of energy in fruitless efforts to fight off or control these emotions. It's kind of like quicksand. The more you struggle, the more quickly you sink. If you could just relax and actually lie forward or backward onto the quicksand (the exact opposite of what you feel like doing!), you'd find that you could float and get free of the trap. It's the same with fear. If you quit struggling with it, you're far more likely to find a way to get free.

Another good metaphor for this principle is Chinese handcuffs, or finger traps, those slender tubes woven from straw. You can stick a finger of each hand into the two ends relatively easily, but when you try to pull your fingers out, the tube tightens around your fingers and traps them. The harder you try to pull your fingers out, the more the tube tightens. Even if you never played with a finger trap as a kid, you can probably imagine how they work. You need to push in a little; this expands the tube enough to let your fingers slip out.

There's a profound life lesson in this little toy: That which you resist persists.

I've heard many stories of this principle at work in people's lives, and perhaps you've experienced it in your own life. The converse is also true: People have saved their lives by turning in the direction of a skid on ice, turning toward a deadly tailspin in an airplane, or diving deep into the most terrifying current in a white-water river.

The Keeper Hole

My friend Walt, an expert kayaker, took his boat down the creek in front of my house some years ago. This was right after a big storm, and as he went over a small waterfall, he found it was much more dangerous than he'd ever seen it. He got stuck at the bottom of it in what river runners call a keeper hole—a deadly current that captures anything that comes into it and rarely lets it go.

Though he tried several times to get to the surface and paddle out, Walt couldn't get free. He finally kicked out of the kayak and tried to swim out, but the keeper hole wouldn't let him free. He was becoming hypothermic and exhausted. He was drowning. In a last desperate effort, he did something that felt crazy. Swimming to the surface one more time, he took a big gulp of air and dove down into the current's deepest, coldest, darkest, scariest depths and swam with it for all he was worth. After a few seconds that probably seemed like an eternity, he found himself being drawn to the surface about twenty feet away, free from the keeper hole.

He saved his life by an act of radical acceptance—diving into what he feared the most. In the same way, turning toward and being with difficult thoughts and emotions has the power to transform and even save our lives. By turning toward these thoughts and emotions when they arise in meditation practice, we gradually cultivate the strength and courage to turn toward and be with scary situations in interpersonal relationships. This is one of the most healing elements of mindfulness meditation. It's not that we can meditate fear, anxiety, or pain away; it's that we come into a different relationship with these inescapable aspects of the human condition and find new ways to respond to our fears, rather than react to them with aversion.

Shyness and Aversion

Aversion is not just the nemesis of the shy and socially anxious; it's a source of suffering in every human life. But we could say that aversion is like the theme song of all people who consider themselves shy. It's certainly the central dynamic and can even be used as a synonym for shyness. As discussed in chapter 1, aversion is a deep instinct, hardwired into us as part of the fight, flight, or freeze self-protection system. It works pretty well when it drives you to avoid that house on the corner that has the mean dog, but it's ineffective, at best, when it comes to avoiding thoughts, emotions, and interpersonal relationships. When you try to avoid other people, you have to give up much that you want from others. Plus, the very effort it takes to escape and avoid people actually elevates interpersonal relationships to such a level of importance that you end up feeling consumed by them anyway.

Aversion to other people can be sparked by many things—their political orientation, religion, taste in clothes or music, or even their cologne. Almost anything can get under your skin and provoke the fight, flight, or freeze reaction. As explored in chapter 1, the fear body is conditioned by experiences of aversion and then reacts automatically when exposed to similar situations. If it's been programmed to go off around people in general, it can create many problems for you, including firing off even around people you'd like to be close to. This biological mechanism of shyness in your mind and body could be called the anxiety-based avoidance system.

This type of avoidance is one of the greatest sources of suffering in shyness and social anxiety. While it would appear that you're trying to protect yourself by avoiding interpersonal relationships, what you're really trying to avoid is the experience of anxiety and fear itself. As a boy I could outrun bullies, but I couldn't outrun my own fear or self-recriminations, which grew louder and more painful the more I ran.

The implication is simple and straightforward: You can pretty much avoid being in significant relationships with other people, but you can't avoid being with your mind. The truth is, you get hurt when you're in relationships, and you get hurt for want of relationships. Pain is unavoidable, and a part of all relationships. Because you've chosen to work on your shyness, your principal intention must shift from avoidance mode to learning how to come to terms with hurt. Perhaps this skill is also part of what makes great athletes; it's not that their muscles and joints don't hurt, but that they've found a way to cope with pain by using it as a guide rather than shrinking from it.

Exercise:
Investigating Social Aversion

This exercise will help you investigate some of your own avoidance patterns. For the next week, be aware of your experience of aversion in interpersonal relationship as it's occurring, and record these events in your shyness journal at the end of the day, or throughout the day if you're able. Use the form below as a template. Fill in as many details as possible about the thoughts, emotions, sensations, and reactions you experience with each incidence of social aversion. (For a version of this form you can download and print out, see my website, www.mindful livingprograms.com.)

Instances of Social Aversion				
	Thoughts	Emotions	Sensations	Reactions
Monday				
Tuesday				
Wednesday				
Thursday				
Friday				
Saturday				
Sunday				

getting unstuck

Relationships truly are fraught with peril and are guaranteed to bring much pain into your life, but the only way you'll ever learn to cope with interpersonal suffering is by turning toward and working within relationships. You can't wait for the anxiety to go away and only then take some risks with relationships. You'll get there only by cultivating courage, which can be defined as facing what scares you even though you feel afraid. You may fear that you'll mess up and blow it, but only by failing and recovering can you learn how to tolerate your own missteps, or those of others. Of course you will fall flat on your face sometimes, but you'll find that every time you get up and begin again, it hurts a little less and you learn a little more. Your meditation practice is a place where you can prepare for failing and beginning again a lot, since failing to stay with the focus of your practice and returning to it is a large part of practice.

When you spend more time in awareness through your meditation practice, you can see that it's possible to witness thoughts as just thoughts and become less compelled by them. You discover that if you can sit with an itch and not scratch it, it actually fades away on its own. You can turn toward greedy and lusty thoughts and fearful and anxious thoughts and not do anything at all with them, and they too fade away. The whole parade of thoughts can begin to disperse when the mind sees that you aren't that attached to its performances. As you sit with your thoughts, you can see the gross inaccuracies, exaggerations, judgments, and delusions they spin. You can feel all of the emotional and physical reactions and choose to simply let them be and let them go with a spirit of acceptance. In such a state of mind, even anxiety can't find a place to stick. Without anyone to resist it or try to control it, anxiety too can disperse. This is how you grow in acceptance and stop the fruitless struggle to avoid everyone and everything that scares you.

Acceptance—opening to be with things as they are—is the way to stop struggling against what is and embark on a path toward healing and love. Remember the finger traps, and that important life lesson that what you resist persists? One reason it's so important to identify what you're resisting and where you're stuck is that this informs you of where you need to practice unconditional acceptance.

• Discoveries on the Path: *Carla's Story*

It was the third night in a week that Carla had turned to look at the clock at 3:30 in the morning. She was angry at herself again and couldn't go to sleep. Fuming, tossing, and turning, she couldn't get comfortable for more than a few minutes. "How could I be so stupid?" she said to herself for the umpteenth time. "I'm never going to have a boyfriend!"

At lunchtime on Monday, John, a coworker, had come to her desk and asked what she was doing on Saturday, and whether she'd like to go out for dinner and a movie. In a knee-jerk response, she told him thanks, but she had other plans. She turned over again and stared at the clock. "How could I be so stupid!" She couldn't push the thoughts out of her mind.

Carla liked John. He was nice and smiled at her every time he saw her. She would love to go out with him, but she didn't even think before she said no. "When I go in tomorrow, I'm going to go over to John's desk and ask him if he'd like to go to lunch with me." Her heart began beating wildly at just the thought of it, and she knew she would never, ever do something like that. Lying there feeling her heart pound, she remembered what she had learned a couple of weeks ago in her meditation class: "The body is a place to ground when you're swamped with thoughts and emotions." She decided to try it and concentrated on her heart beating in her chest. She tried to feel everything she could feel in her chest—the tightness, the shallow, rapid breaths. She tried to be with every sensation as best as she could and could see how all of this came from her anger and her self-blame.

The more she stayed with the sensations, the less she was blaming herself. In a few minutes she noticed that her breath was changing and her heart wasn't beating so hard. The quieter her heart became, the quieter her mind became. As her breath dropped into her belly, a big sadness came over her. She placed her hand on her heart and thought, "I can't help it if I get scared." As she was drifting off to sleep, Carla told herself, "He's the nicest guy in the office, and I think he likes me. If he ever asks me again, I'll say yes."

In the morning Carla wondered if her anger was just a way to avoid her sadness and realized that her sadness arose from her fear that she would never be able to change and would always be alone. She found that she could relate to these feelings with understanding and a measure of acceptance. She had found a way to befriend fear and anger and even managed to write a few words in her diary before she left for work: "I forgive myself. My body is a refuge."

Carla felt this experience was the beginning of a whole new path in working with her fear and anger. She found it comforting to regard her pounding heart as an expression of a story and the emotions that story evoked. She could see how these emotions arose, and she had found a way to relate to her fear rather then run from it. She was no longer the person who was entangled in her thoughts and emotions; she was the person who was witnessing them with compassion.

Turning Toward Life with Loving Kindness

Carla's experience shows what can happen when you shift from fighting your thoughts and emotions to being with them in your body with compassion and awareness. She found that her body could be like a compass, helping her get her bearings when she got lost in the wilderness of self-blame and self-hatred. It could show her the way home to equanimity and loving-kindness.

Loving-kindness is a gift of acceptance and compassion for yourself and for others. The practice of loving-kindness involves cultivating sincere friendliness toward yourself and others and not only wishing the very best for yourself, but giving your best to yourself and others. Love and kindness are the arms that cradle you as you face and feel the things that you need to in your meditation practice, and in your relationships. It's especially important for you to cultivate this practice if you've rarely extended this attitude toward yourself. This marriage of wisdom and love, mind and heart, can carry you through life's darkest moments. It's like a balm for the soul and a way to calm the harsh and attacking self-critic.

As in all practices, you can only start from where you are. If you are shy, it's very likely that your attitude toward yourself has rarely been

compassionate and kind. Be patient with yourself; these kinds of attitudes don't change overnight. You may need to start with small steps,
just wetting your lips at the wellspring of loving-kindness and offering
yourself some small measure of compassion for the suffering you've had
to bear in your life. Think of your fear and pain as similar to those of a
child who has awakened from a nightmare and needs your loving care
and kindness. Turn to and care for this suffering; hold it with tenderness and compassion. That's a good place to begin. You can return to
the well of loving-kindness and wet your lips with this water of life
again and again. One day you'll feel ready to take a sip, and eventually
a drink.

Like a wise and loving healer in your own heart, loving-kindness
will show you a way to freedom and support you on your path through
the aversion that shyness and social anxiety provokes. So how do you
get there? How do you look for and open to these expressions of healing,
which already lie within you? This next practice will help draw these
healing energies forth.

mindfulness practice:
Loving-Kindness Practice

Take your seat in the place you've created for your meditation practice
with the intention to be fully present for this practice for thirty minutes.
Offer yourself some appreciation for giving yourself this time to practice
self-compassion and loving-kindness. As well as you can, settle into this
moment through your mindful breathing practice and be present.

1. Bring your awareness into the vicinity of your heart, and
   expand the sense of appreciating yourself for giving yourself this practice. Know that this is a gift of love. Consider
   everything you've taken on to invest yourself in healing,
   and acknowledge the time you've spent in reading, self-
   exploration, and mindfulness practices. Also consider the
   unhappiness and suffering that led you to this work. Open
   your heart to itself—and yourself—with compassion.

2. With heartfelt understanding and goodwill, offer these intentions, or phrase them however feels right to you, resting with those intentions for a few breaths before going to the next: "May I be free from fear and suffering. May I be peaceful and at ease. May I be healthy in mind and body. May I be happy in this life, just as it is."

3. Repeating these self-soothing words to yourself three times, take these kind words and intentions into the vicinity of your heart. By infusing your own heart with this kind of love, you will gradually find that you can offer these same kind and compassionate words to others.

4. When you're ready, offer these same intentions to each of these recipients in turn, just as you've offered them to yourself: a teacher or mentor, a dear friend or loved one, your community, an adversary, and then everyone, everywhere. "May you be free from fear and suffering. May you be peaceful and at ease. May you be healthy in mind and body. May you be happy in this life, just as it is." Take your time. Open your heart to give and receive loving-kindness as deeply as you can.

5. Please give yourself thirty minutes for your loving-kindness practice and conclude with some mindful breathing. Thank yourself for doing this.

Notes to Yourself

Take some time to write about your loving-kindness practice in your journal. Please include your reflections about any resistance that came up for you in this practice and how you worked with it. What emotions came up? Were there memories or dreams or hopes that this practice evoked?

Empathetic Joy

Empathetic joy occurs when you find your heart opening with appreciation and empathy for the joy you witness in others. You'll find this kind of joy very helpful if you need something to prime the pump of loving-kindness for yourself. Start looking for expressions of loving-kindness in the world around you. A baby is a good place to look, particularly if she's with a grandma who is all goo-goo eyes over her. (Grandma can be a pretty rich source too!) Keep your eye out for young lovers, old lovers, and kids with puppies or kittens. Notice the many ways they express loving-kindness. It can be contagious, and you may learn how to give it to yourself by watching how it is given by others.

the value of shyness

Having spent so much time exploring the elements of shyness and social anxiety that create suffering in your life, it's good that you've finally arrived at this point where you can experience and acknowledge the value of self-compassion and loving-kindness. Bringing this kind of awareness to yourself as you face painful and difficult emotions enables you to see them and respond to them rather than be controlled and compelled by them. The healing power of mindfulness arises from the openhearted, compassionate awareness you bring to yourself as you turn toward your own suffering and to others as you witness their suffering. This perspective changes everything.

I now view my many years of shyness as having given me a great gift, for without shyness I might never have found compassion and loving-kindness. My feelings of shyness led me to meditation and to a deep exploration of the inward dimensions of being human. It led me to be with myself and care for myself in ways that no one else could. Shyness has become the source of empathy and compassion in my heart for others who feel frightened and alone, because I can see that their suffering is no different from my own. This has helped me grow in sensitivity, tenderness, and kindness, and I treasure these gifts. Strange as it may seem, I've actually come to feel grateful for shyness in my life!

Not only can shyness be valuable for driving this sort of growth and self-inquiry, it also has qualities that can be endearing. Consider the words "demure" and "modest," which are sometimes used as synonyms for "shyness." In some cultures shyness is prized and people even act shy to be seen as more attractive. Understand that in working skillfully with shyness you can choose to enhance those qualities of shyness that you appreciate just as you diminish those that create pain and suffering. This calls for gaining more perspective, clarity, and equanimity in how you regard yourself.

the floodlight of awareness

In our work together so far, you've learned a lot about shyness and social anxiety and how mindfulness can help. You've explored the attitudes and fundamentals of mindfulness meditation and have had many opportunities to experience concentration, or "spotlight," mindfulness practices. The investment you've made in these practices has helped you cultivate a quality of awareness that can illuminate all the moments of your life. This awareness is something much more than the practices themselves and is the benefit of practice, just like increased strength is the benefit of rigorous exercise.

The following practice will enable you to work with this wide-open kind of awareness more deliberately. This practice is called choiceless awareness because it's much more like a floodlight than a spotlight. It's the most fluid and spacious practice of mindfulness meditation, and it's also something you can bring to everything you do. When you're working with shyness and avoidance patterns, this broad kind of awareness can benefit you a lot in interpersonal relationships by illuminating things just as they are, without the cognitive distortions that can sometimes color social interactions.

One of the fruits of choiceless awareness is a clear recognition of the impermanent and ever-changing nature of all things. Breath by breath, moment by moment, you are always changing and the world is always changing. No two breaths are alike, and no two moments are alike. Give yourself a lot of slack in beginning this practice; because it doesn't employ a particular meditative object, such as the felt sense of the breath, it's very challenging. Choiceless awareness is sometimes described as awareness of awareness itself, and in practice it doesn't even involve a sense of self or the familiar sense of personal identity—of being the one who is experiencing awareness. Awareness itself becomes the object of practice as well as the subject of practice. Take your time and take it easy. It's a state of awareness that you'll need to develop with time.

mindfulness practice:
Choiceless Awareness

Give yourself at least thirty minutes for this practice. Choose a place that's as quiet as possible and where you won't be disturbed. Sit upright on a chair without leaning against the chair's back, or on a meditation cushion in a way that feels like your back can be well supported by your posture. Be balanced and at ease and neither too rigid nor too relaxed. See if you can find a posture where your head, neck, and body feel aligned and there's a sense of comfort and dignity in your body.

1. Close your eyes or leave them slightly open with a relaxed, unfocused, and downward gaze. Give yourself ten minutes of mindful breathing practice. Follow your breath into the present moment and offer yourself some appreciation and thanks for taking this time to grow in mindfulness.

2. When you feel present with your breath, allow the sensations of breathing to recede into the background of your awareness while you direct your attention to hearing, noticing that sounds come and go just as breaths come and go. Each has a beginning and an end and is a distinct event in itself. Being aware of any judgments or interpretations about the sounds you hear and letting them be. Notice if you contract around some sounds or feel a sense of releasing with others. Let all sounds be a way for you to show up and be present. Being present for sounds for about five minutes.

3. Expand your awareness of sensations by turning your attention to your body as a whole and noticing, as your way to be present, whatever bodily sensation is most prominent. Being with changing sensations of the body for the next five minutes.

4. Shift your practice once again, this time to mindfulness of the mind. Notice thoughts and emotions as they arise and use each mental event as a way to show up and be present. Notice that each thought or emotion, like each breath, has a beginning and an end and is a temporary event. You may also notice that some thoughts and emotions evoke strong feelings of aversion or attraction. If it's helpful to acknowledge your experience by noting thoughts and emotions at first, please do so: "planning," "worrying," "judging," "sadness," "joy," and so on. You may also find that observations arise like "positive thought" or "negative emotion." Being present for mental and emotional states as they come and go for the next five minutes.

5. Expand your practice now to begin choiceless awareness by first using the changing experience of sensations, thoughts, or emotions as a means to be present. Employ whatever experience seems most prominent at any given moment. Being present with whatever arises and residing in the present moment with attention and without an agenda. Stay with this practice for a minute or two, then release your attention from these meditative objects and see if you can simply be awareness itself. Consider this to be a place a little like the sky—a vast space that provides the space for clouds that come and go, appear and disappear. Like clouds, sensations, thoughts, or emotions may appear, but you are the sky that contains them. The nature of this awareness is nonconcentration and spacious. Let your attention expand to take in the whole spectrum of your mind and body with kind acceptance. Allow whatever arises to simply be. Like the sky, opening to all things and refusing nothing. Without judging, without clinging, being receptive and accepting of everything. Be as the sky for a few minutes, as well as you can, resting in awareness, relaxed and alert.

6. Conclude this practice by returning to mindfulness of the breath for five minutes. As you bring your practice to a close, thank yourself once again for taking this time to care for yourself and grow in mindfulness.

Notes to Yourself

Take a few minutes to write in your journal about what you experienced during your choiceless awareness practice. Could you get a glimpse of the simple experience of pure awareness? Could you get a sense of the fluidity of this practice and the changing nature of your habitual sense of self?

schedule practice

Please take a moment now to schedule daily mindfulness practice with loving-kindness and choiceless awareness. It will serve you best to practice every day and to take these practices into your interpersonal relationships informally yet very deliberately at different times of the day. Try practicing in neutral places like a museum or grocery store and in more challenging places like a classroom or your workplace

Up to this point, you've had a chance to experience both formal and informal mindfulness practices. You've learned and practiced mindfulness of the breath and body, the body scan, walking meditation, yoga, observing and noting thoughts and emotions, loving-kindness meditation, choiceless awareness, and more. It's important that you invest yourself in these practices, perhaps over a period of a couple of months, so that you have a solid foundation in mindfulness to bring into interpersonal relationships. Vary the practices and make them your own, and know that this is an unfolding process that develops as you go along. Your mindfulness will grow month after month and year after year as you practice. In the meanwhile, every hour and minute, indeed, every moment you invest in cultivating mindfulness will help you.

If you'd like, give yourself two months of personal mindfulness practice before beginning the interpersonal mindfulness practices in the rest of the book. Be sure to schedule daily practice. Many people find it helpful to do both stillness practices and movement practices daily. If you have chosen to participate in the MPTS Program and are following the daily schedule provided in the workbook, you are already well into your two-month program. Whatever type of practice you choose, know that it will build a foundation of mindfulness that will provide a secure home base from which you can take risks and care for yourself as you face the difficult and challenging world of social encounters—the work we'll take on in part 4 of this book.

a calling to remember

This chapter has given you a close and mindful look at escape and avoidance. You've tallied up some of the cost you pay when you give in to these urges that arise from aversion, and you've looked at how this creates suffering in your life. Remember, that which you resist persists, whereas the things you turn toward transform you.

From the very beginning of your work with this book, you've explored how mindfulness and compassion can help you overcome the suffering inherent in shyness and also help you to discover a new sense of wholeness and freedom. By practicing mindfulness, you've seen that it's possible to make room for fear and anxiety and still remain present, and you've begun to see and feel for yourself the benefits of being present for the experience of your life.

In the chapters ahead, you'll deepen your mindfulness practice and apply it specifically to those elements of shyness and social anxiety that create the greatest problems in your life. You'll learn ways to be mindful in relationships and develop mindfulness practices that you can apply in interpersonal relationships.

Part IV
interpersonal mindfulness

Willing to experience aloneness,
I discover connection everywhere;
Turning to face my fear,
I meet the warrior who lives within;
Opening to my loss,
I gain the embrace of the universe;
Surrendering into emptiness,
I find fullness without end.
Each condition I flee from pursues me,
Each condition I welcome transforms me,
And becomes itself transformed
Into its radiant jewel-like essence.
I bow to the one who has made it so,
Who has crafted this Master Game;
To play it is purest delight—
To honor its form, true devotion.
                    —Jennifer Paine Welwood, "Unconditional"

cultivating mindfulness in interpersonal relationships

To dare is to lose one's footing momentarily. Not to dare is to lose oneself.

—Søren Kierkegaard

Remember the teaching of the stinging nettle plant, in chapter 6? Sometimes the very things that hurt and scare us also offer a healing balm. In regard to shyness and social anxiety, this means finding healing by turning toward and looking within interpersonal relationships. In the parlance of psychology this is called *exposure*, and it's an important part of cognitive behavioral therapy for the treatment of shyness.

Much of the work that you've done thus far in this book was necessary to bring you to this point. The practices you've cultivated on your own have provided you with vital skills that you'll need to proceed with the exercises ahead and navigate the world of interpersonal relationships:

- Being present

- Recognizing and letting go of judgments

- Recognizing and letting go of striving

- Recognizing thoughts and not identifying with them

- Recognizing emotions and not identifying with them

- Caring for yourself and others with compassion and loving-kindness

One of the discoveries you may someday make in meditation practice is a state of mind where you can just be. There is a sense of calm and spacious awareness in this place. Consider this the still point or home base that you can operate from as you make mindful excursions into the world of interpersonal relationships. One of the great things about mindfulness is that it's portable; this awareness can go with you wherever you go. When you're navigating the sometimes rough waters of relationships, you can periodically eddy out in still points of being. You can stay with challenges to the edge of your skills or endurance, and then rest to recenter when you need to. And with each new excursion, you can extend your skill.

To find a sense of equanimity in relationships may have seemed impossible before you started cultivating mindfulness in your life—and it may still be difficult now. Interpersonal mindfulness is a very challenging work for anyone, even after practicing meditation for a long time. But this is what you've been working toward: being mindful in your relationships and discovering greater connectedness and fulfillment in being with others. This is why a daily meditation practice is so important. It will help you find and cultivate mindfulness and compassion in your own heart that you can extend to relationships.

In this chapter, you'll translate the skills you've been cultivating by yourself into the external worlds you share with others. You'll do this by way of intentional exposure to relationships that bring up feelings of shyness and anxiety.

mindful connection

Research shows that we humans have built-in qualities that support connectedness and intimacy. Daniel Siegel, MD (2007b) presents research into interpersonal neurobiology that indicates we're hardwired for empathy, attunement, and resonance in interpersonal relationships. *Attunement* is tuning in to or attending to the emotions of others, and *resonance* is "feeling felt," which arises out of attunement. You might consider attunement to be like tuning your guitar to match your friend's guitar, and resonance to be when a string on your guitar vibrates in response to your friend's guitar. In other words, we have brain circuitry that enables us to feel connected to (or disconnected from) others and to sense and join in what they feel.

Early childhood development has an enormous influence on this sense of connectedness, but it appears that the capacity for attunement and resonance is built in and, further, that it is malleable and can be developed by mindfulness practices. Dr. Siegel suggests that mindfulness meditation helps cultivate the capacity for empathy and connectedness by enabling us to calm ourselves and become more deeply attuned to our own feelings, and thereby become better able to attune to the feelings of others. This takes intimacy to a whole new level. A funny thing is that you can read the word "intimacy" as "into me see," and it's certainly true that if I can see inside of me, I may be able to see inside of you.

Anyone who spends any amount of time in meditation practice quickly encounters an internal dialogue rife with the concepts, prejudices, preferences, and emotional reactions that preoccupy and fill our consciousness most of the time. Noticing where your mind is and then returning to quiet watching is something that happens quite a lot in meditation practice. Sometimes called *recentering*, this is a skill you can develop in your personal mindfulness practice and then bring into interpersonal mindfulness practice. If you can recenter on your own, in the private world of your own mind and body, you'll be better equipped to recenter with other people.

The research reviewed by Dr. Siegel indicates that long-term meditators form neural integration networks between the prefrontal lobe of the brain, an area associated with abilities to self-calm, and other parts of the brain that are associated with anxiety and fear reactions, such as the amygdala, which is recognized as the seat of survival instincts like anger, fear, and aggression. The resulting band of neurofibers can transmit an enormous amount of energy and information via neurotransmitters like GABA (gamma-aminobutyric acid), enabling us to soothe and regulate reactive emotional states and better respond to difficult life situations with flexibility and reflection. At a conference in 2007, Dr. Siegel referred to this as "flooding our amygdala with GABA goo" (Siegel 2007a). Meditation helps us transform difficult emotions at their roots, thereby allowing us to develop and maintain equanimity and connectedness in relationships with others.

developing interpersonal mindfulness

The intention of interpersonal mindfulness is to show up in relationships and be fully present without judging or striving with others. When listening to others, you simply listen to them. When looking at others, you are able to simply see them. This makes you a better receiver of the information the other person is sending to you. There is just this one moment, this one immediate experience that you are sharing together. Extraneous material from your own thoughts, emotions, and sensations will enter this moment and can and will lead you away from attending to the person you're engaged with. The invitation is to acknowledge these distractions, let them be, and return to the interaction.

Imagine you're sitting with a few people who are talking about their dream vacations and you're the only one who hasn't shared anything yet. Though people are still talking, you realize that soon someone is probably going to ask you what your dream vacation is. Suddenly you get the idea that your dream of going to Disney World will sound childish and stupid next to the European and Caribbean vacations the others have mentioned. You become so swept up in your self-doubting thoughts and feelings that you don't even hear what anyone else is saying. You start flooding with anxious thoughts, your heart starts beating faster, and you feel the familiar urge to escape.

However, the mindful awareness you've developed allows you to realize you've left the actual conversation and entered the fear body. This is a moment where you can apply the mindfulness skills you've been cultivating. Noticing your anxious thoughts and sensations, you acknowledge them. Then, returning to the present moment via the breath moving in your belly, you let those thoughts and sensations be and reinvest yourself in listening intently to what your companions are saying. When you refocus into the here and now, you are no longer facing a group of critical people in some future scenario, but simply listening to one woman talking. You might note her exuberance as she describes her dream vacation. You're just sitting, listening, and enjoying her exuberance. You begin to calm down as you once again contact that place of quiet presence you've found in your meditation practice.

The work is in becoming sensitive and compassionate to yourself independent of relationships, and then being sensitive and compassionate with yourself and others within relationships and interactions. It's certainly not a matter of toughing it out or shutting down your emotions and forcing yourself to endure things you hate. Remember the wisdom in yoga practice about exploring the edge of a stretch? By waiting at the edge with patience and without trying to escape, you discover a release rather than forcing it. You can gradually come to terms with some of the most distressing elements of interpersonal relationships in the same way. When you're with others, you approach and stay near the edge of your social anxiety and fear deliberately. Gradually, you'll develop a different relationship with these emotions and the people you're interacting with. As with the release you feel in yoga, you'll experience greater ease and relaxation in relationships, and ultimately become more attuned and resonant with other people.

As you befriend your own difficult emotions, you'll be in a better position to encounter the difficult emotions of others and come to realize that your feelings aren't fundamentally different from everybody else's. This recognition in itself can help free you from the prison of self-consciousness as you discover that you aren't really alone. All human beings suffer and have to cope with emotional pain. From this deep knowing of our mutual suffering, compassion arises.

Through interpersonal mindfulness practices, you can learn how you create suffering in your relationships and then learn how to stop doing these things. If this concept seems daunting, know that the person you are now, just beginning to work with these interpersonal practices, is not the same person you will be at the end of this journey. There will be hardships and triumphs, but as you practice you'll develop new skills to manage distress, experience empathy, and feel compassion for others.

Personal Suffering and Interpersonal Suffering

Meditation teacher and author Gregory Kramer, Ph.D., has developed some powerful tools for interpersonal meditation practice as well as some clear insights into personal and interpersonal suffering and distress. I'm grateful for his permission to paraphrase a little of his work here, as well as his gracious assistance in reviewing it. In this chapter, we'll look at some of the basic elements of what he calls "insight dialogue," but the best resource for this practice is his book *Insight Dialogue: The Interpersonal Path to Freedom* (Kramer 2008).

It's helpful to understand the principal sources of suffering in interpersonal relationships. In the first two years of human life, the brain adds synapses at a rate that will never again be replicated. At this time, our earliest experiences with others creates a sense of self that feels separate from everyone else. From this newly emergent sense of "me," you see things with your eyes and feel things with your skin. You feel your pleasure and your pain. You discover that there are some things you like and want and some you don't like and don't want. This new and independent sense of self is regarded by psychologists as normal ego development, yet it is also the source of desire and all personal suffering.

During this time you also discover feelings of being safe and connected to some people and wary of and disconnected from others. The ego or sense of self that develops at this time will be informed by these feelings and will accompany you and color much of what you think, feel, and do for the rest of your life. If you learn that you need to be an entertainer to get the attention you long for, you'll entertain. If you learn that it's not safe to be seen and heard, you'll learn to be quietly invisible by developing complex patterns of avoidance and self-protection. This is where our personality patterns develop.

These earliest experiences set in motion a pattern of wanting and not wanting, of seeking and avoiding in your relationships with other people. This is the source of what Dr. Kramer calls interpersonal suffering. You can suffer in your interpersonal relationships when you experience either desire for or fear of another.

Given your shyness, much of your life may be colored by the sense of being separate from and averse to others, even if there's still much that you want from them. The suffering of shyness is kind of a double whammy—it arises from both aversion and desire.

Dr. Kramer distinguishes social suffering from interpersonal suffering, classifying interpersonal suffering as that which arises between two people and social suffering as that which arises in relation to groups of people. Many of us first experienced social suffering when we started going to school and no longer felt protected in the safety and familiarity of our family. Suddenly there's a sense of "me" as separate from them, rather than "we." Within this new social arena, both desire and aversion will arise, along with self-judgment and self-blame.

• Discoveries on the Path: *Kevin's Story*

As Kevin began to explore his shy feelings in meditation practice, he made some important discoveries about how he came to be so anxious in groups. He kept having aversive memories of being the apple of his mother's eye. "It may seem like a good thing that my mom thought I was adorable," he told us one day at our meditation group, "but it certainly didn't feel like a good thing to me! She dressed me up like a living doll to be shown off to everyone she encountered. I hated this, but it didn't seem to matter how I felt about it; the show went on at home, in stores, at restaurants, everywhere."

Kevin mostly escaped being the center of his mom's show when he started going to school. But he soon realized that he was carrying this problem along with him, as he found himself as the center of his own show. Almost immediately, he felt separate and different from the other kids. "I felt anxious and self-conscious. I still felt like I was the center of attention, but I felt inadequate and weird. It always seemed like it was 'me and them,' and I never got to know anybody, really. I worried about what other kids thought about me, and I felt like I was different. I was always self-conscious and never seemed to fit in. Even now, I always feel like somebody's watching me." As time went on, Kevin tried to be the opposite of his flamboyant and exhibitionistic mother, who loved being on stage. He tried to be invisible and avoid drawing attention to himself.

One day Kevin announced to our meditation group that he had made a painful discovery: that he and his mom weren't so different at all. "It gives me the creeps, but I think I'm just like her! We're both on imaginary stages in front of imaginary audiences that exist mostly in our own minds. On her stage she's a star and wants to be seen, and on my stage I'm a geek and want to disappear. Either way, it's all a big, crazy delusion. There's no stage and there is no audience. We've both got our own imaginary show going called 'It's All About Me!'

Interpersonal Desire and Aversion

The cause of interpersonal suffering is the same as the cause of personal suffering: desire. The only difference is that in interpersonal suffering, our needs and desires are directed toward others. Desire has two sides: the things that we want and the things that we don't want. In interpersonal suffering, we experience this as wanting something from others and pursuing them to get it, or not wanting anything from others and trying to avoid the people who want something from us.

Perhaps not surprisingly, these two energies are often magnetically attracted to one another. Those who desire and want things from others tend to get together with people who just want to be left alone. This keeps those who are seeking on the path of seeking, and those who are avoiding on the path of avoiding. Partnerships formed of these two opposing energies can become a perennial source of intrigue, entertainment, and distress as each person faithfully plays out their respective roles of seeking or avoiding.

We can't just stop wanting and not wanting things from others, but if we can bring enough light into interpersonal desire and fear, we may be able to make more conscious choices to diminish the suffering these forces cause in our lives. For example, you may look deeply into your yearning in regard to other people and discover that you crave something only you can give yourself. An example is wanting to be admired so you can feel good about yourself. If you look to others for this, it's a losing proposition, because when you depend on the admiration of others to feel good, you're likely to fear that they might withhold it.

Sometimes we discover that we want something that could only have been given by our primary caregivers when we were very young. Unfortunately, the time is long past when it could have been given. In this case, what's called for is grieving that loss, rather than seeking that infantile kind of love in another adult. Although difficult, it can be extremely liberating to look deeply into what you want and fear from others. The light of compassionate awareness may itself dispel unrealistic desires and fears and set you free from unnecessary suffering.

There are three basic hungers. The first is the desire for pleasure, which comes with a corresponding aversion to pain. "Make me feel good" and "Don't ever scare me or hurt me" can take many forms and fill our interpersonal relationships. The second basic hunger is to have our very existence confirmed by others, which comes with a corresponding fear of invisibility. In Kevin's story, you may recognize this particular hunger in the performances of his mother, who wanted to be seen and admired and was afraid of not being noticed. The third basic hunger is the desire to escape and not be seen or known by other people, which comes with a corresponding fear of being seen. You may recognize this pattern in Kevin's personality or in your own efforts to avoid and escape interpersonal relationships. Most people with social anxiety probably have a great deal of this third hunger.

Insight Dialogue

Insight dialogue (Kramer 2008) is a powerful vehicle for formal and informal interpersonal meditation practice that has helped many people free themselves from interpersonal suffering. It's composed of six actions, which may be employed in formal practice or utilized any-where, anytime: pause, open, relax, trust emergence, listen deeply, and speak the truth. Let's take a closer look at each of these intentions.

Pause is a reminder to yourself, given inwardly, to stop for a little while. But what stops? It's the habit mind, the compelling intrigue of your own thoughts. So pause is a call to stop and shift fully into awareness, into the here and now. At this moment, you may notice what thoughts, emotions, and sensations are coursing through you, with all of their elements of desire and aversion. Pausing can illuminate what's happening with you as you listen or talk to others. Pausing corresponds to medita-tion practice itself.

Relax is an intention you bring to the tension you find in your body when you settle into the pause. You may notice what the tensing is related to as you feel into the tightness or contraction with curiosity and acceptance. With a scary thought, you pause, relax, and begin again. You let everything be and invite the part of your body that's tense to let go. You turn toward whatever you're holding in your body and simultaneously toward your mind with loving-kindness and com-passion. You let it be and let it go, again and again.

Open involves extending the acceptance and mindfulness you've been cultivating in your personal meditation practice to the external world, and specifically to those you're engaged with. It's an agenda-free receptivity toward the external world that may be first cultivated personally, independent of others. Opening to nature can be a good place to begin, providing a context in which you can feel very safe in opening. You can open to a forest or an ocean, the sky or the desert, or even a flower. You might go for a walk in the rain or find a place where you can open to a star-filled night.

Trust emergence invites you to remain poised in the open space that you've created by pausing and relaxing. You allow whatever may come up, without rushing in to fill the space out of some need or discomfort. Think of it as trusting that something will emerge when the moment is right, or trusting whatever emerges, without clinging to the past or preconceptions about the future. In social contexts, it means allowing the conversation to form within the interaction without trying to control or manipulate it. Trust emergence is being present, on purpose, in this ever-changing moment, with acceptance of whatever arises.

Listen deeply means becoming a receptive field that receives the words and feelings expressed by another person. The invitation is to listen with kindness and compassion and allow yourself to be touched by another human being. This kind of listening is patient, nonjudging, and free from personal agendas. The attitude of listening deeply is a willingness to feel with and experience the thoughts and feelings of another human being without *personalizing* what you hear, meaning misinterpreting it on the basis of your personal concepts or preferences.

Speak the truth means to be honest with the person you're interacting with. It's straight talk in the sense of saying things as you perceive them to be. The intention is to express what's useful and appropriate with attention to goodwill and without cruelty. This is the union of mindfulness with virtue, morality, and mutuality. Is what you are saying true? Is it beneficial? Is it kind? Is it offered in goodwill? It's important to consider all of these questions, as speaking the truth calls for not only honesty, but also a sincere intention not to injure others. A helpful guideline is to consider the golden rule and speak to others as you would like to be spoken to.

You can use any of these powerful tools for interpersonal mindfulness, either singly or in combination, in your day-to-day communications with others. The following exercises will help you use four of these tools—pause, relax, open, and listen deeply—to investigate your experiences in interpersonal relationships. Using some simple intentions and interactions, you may apply these skills to recognize the ways you create distress in your life with desire and aversion. As the ways you create distress become more evident, you can draw from mindfulness, acceptance, and loving-kindness to make more skillful choices.

It may be best to stay with each exercise for at least a day before going on to the next. At the end of each day that you practice these skills, take a little time to write in your journal about your experiences. Summarize exactly what you did, where, and with whom, as well as what you discovered. In your journal, acknowledge the sensations, emotions, and thoughts you experienced as you engaged in these interpersonal awareness practices. Also be aware of how you feel as you sit to write about these experiences, and consider writing about that, as well. Know that being present with and for other people is precious and worth every bit of effort you extend., and congratulate yourself for having the courage and commitment to do this.

see for yourself exercise 4:
Exploring Desires Between Us

The next time you're in a group of people and feel a sense of anxiety, pause and recenter into your mindful awareness by employing whatever mindfulness focus works best for you, such as noticing the breath or listening intently. As you become present, do you feel a sense of "me and them," or a sense of "we"? Are your thoughts and emotions pleasant, unpleasant, or neutral? Do they separate you from others or connect you to them?

Check in with your body. What are the strongest sensations you're experiencing? How are your thoughts and emotions connected to those sensations? Then relax. Turn your attention back to those you're with and open. Listen deeply.

Deliberately turning toward others and then back to yourself, again and again, is like kayaking in white water and eddying out. You open to greater risk as you enter the stream of communication, and you stop to mindfully check in with yourself from time to time. As you turn toward yourself, what personal motives do you notice? Are you seeking something from others in any way? As you turn toward others, do you get a sense that anyone is seeking something from you? Can you tell if any of the people you're with are trying to draw attention to themselves or divert it away?

Listen to your companions deeply, doing your best to not only hear their words, but also understand what they're saying and feeling. Extend your very best and warmest intentions to yourself and the others.

see for yourself exercise 5:
Exploring Aversions Between Us

The next time you're in a group of people and feel a sense of anxiety, pause and recenter into your mindful awareness by employing whatever mindfulness focus works best for you. Notice pleasant, unpleasant, or neutral thoughts, emotions, and sensations, then look more deeply to see how different mental and emotional events are connected to sensations.

Relax as much as possible, then notice what you're criticizing, judging, or resenting in yourself or others. What is your experience of fear, anger, or avoidance, and how does it arise? Have you entered into an imaginary future? Return to the breath. Are you caught up in your thoughts and emotions? Return to the now. What are you hearing? What are you seeing? Every time you leave the present, acknowledge where you have gone and return to the now. The more fear and anxiety you feel, the more opportunity you have to recenter. You may notice that in this here and now, in the midst of these experiences, you have the ability to witness your thoughts and feelings, and also have many more options about how to respond to difficult thoughts and feelings beyond the automatic reaction of trying to escape.

Open. Listen deeply. Can you notice whether anyone else in the group is experiencing aversion, perhaps indicated by their words, their silence, or their body language?

See if you can soften and calm your feelings of aversion. Extend your loving-kindness and compassion to yourself and those you're with.

see for yourself exercise 6:
Exploring Judgments Between Us

The next time you experience a sense of being disconnected from someone you're with and feel uncomfortable and anxious, see if you're distancing yourself through judgments. *Pause.* See if you can investigate these judgments more closely. Are you judging the other person? Are you judging yourself? Do you think the other person is judging you? What are the judgments, or what do you imagine they are?

Relax. Open, then inquire whether the judgmental things you've been telling yourself are true. Are you certain? Most of the time you really can't know what's going on in another person's mind, and it can be all too easy to misinterpret the words and actions of others based on judgments you project onto them or imagine them having. How would you be different if you dropped these judgments?

Listen deeply. Staying close to the bare truth of your immediate experience with this person is a way to stop filling the spaces between you with negative interpretations and judgments. See if you can soften and release any judgments you find and extend your loving-kindness and compassion to yourself and to the other person.

mindful communication skills

There are many wonderful books that can help you with communication skills; some of these are listed in the Resources section at the end of this book. For our purposes, let's take a brief look at both sides of the communication process—listening and disclosing—to explore how you can develop perspective for communicating mindfully. Every communication consists of someone talking and someone listening in any given moment. Ideas have to be both sent and received for true communication to have taken place. It's like playing catch.

Mindful Listening

In our harried modern world, so dominated by multitasking, we are often too distracted by our own personal agendas to truly listen to others. Yet there are few things that can foster deep interpersonal connection more than listening mindfully to another person. William Scheick put it well: "Listening intently to another person, sympathetically reflecting on and reflecting back to that person what has been deeply heard beneath the mere surfaces of communication, is a charismatic experience for which there is no adequate word. But the concept of 'grace' comes close, suggesting an intensely felt dispensation from the commonplace. In such rare moments of mutual deep hearing between people, a mind routinely overshadowed by a sense of its lonely isolation is suddenly suffused with a radiant delight. Such delight, like grace, gifts the mind with an experience of the ordinary pierced by the extraordinary" (2002, p. 124).

Like many people who feel shy or socially anxious, you may think you have to become a great talker if you're ever to bridge the gulf between yourself and others. You may worry about what you'll say to others and try to come up with interesting topics of conversation in advance. Let's acknowledge that it won't hurt you to have ready access to a few of these topics if that makes you feel more confident. Sometimes it's comforting to know that you'll have something to say in an awkward silence. But learning to listen mindfully to another person and to discover what William Scheick calls "deep hearing" will help you connect with others in ways that prearranged topics never will. This is profoundly liberating in several ways. Listening like this draws forth responses from you that come from your own deep understanding and may convey a resonance to others from your heart. Mindful listening can help you give others the caring and understanding that you've always longed for and may well invite the same kind of caring for you from those you connect with. Ultimately, it may free you from endless hours of relapsing and worry.

I wish I had figured this out when I felt so shy and socially anxious. I always thought I needed to make such a good impression through what I said—that I had to be more interesting, more entertaining, more expressive. It wasn't until long afterward that I realized the most interesting people are the most interested people. Interest in others helps you find and give expression to your caring heart, and you show your interest by how you listen.

Paradoxically, learning this may get in the way of truly listening, because it's entirely possible to misuse this understanding as a technique to try to avoid sharing anything of yourself and still be interesting to others. But when you use listening in that way, as a strategy, you aren't really interested in the other person, you're attempting to manipulate the situation or person in order to get something from them—namely, their interest in you as a good listener. Used that way, listening can be just another place to hide and can eventually undermine vitality in your relationships.

Mindful listening incorporates the same skills you've cultivated in your individual mindfulness practice. Simply said, mindful listening is being present, open, and receptive to what's being said without judging and without an agenda. Being present in listening means being attentive to the person who is talking, rather than personalizing what you hear or distracting yourself with mental rehearsals of your next comment. Being open corresponds to the curiosity and acceptance you bring into mindfulness practice. Listening without an agenda corresponds to nonstriving.

When you have social anxiety, the way you feel can dominate your communications with others. You can be so caught up in monitoring your fear and your need to make an impression that it's difficult to truly listen to anyone.

Because listening is such an important yet underappreciated and underused art, it may be helpful to explore what listening is, and what it isn't. Here's a list of some of the things that listening isn't about:

- It's not about you.

- It's not about dispelling fear or anxiety.

- It's not about striving to impress someone.

- It's not about getting something from someone.

- It's not about giving something to someone.

- It's not about judging someone.

- It's not about judging yourself.

- It's not about performing.

Now consider this list, which details some of the things that listening *is* about:

- It's about opening and being fully present.

- It's about feeling with another person.

- It's about being present with attention and without an agenda.

- It's about being present with heartfelt curiosity.

- It's about being present without judgment.

- It's about being present with loving-kindness.

- It's about being present with compassion.

Being open and receptive in this way makes it possible to hear not only the words and stories others are sharing, but to empathize with the feelings being expressed. People love to be heard and have their feelings not only felt by another person, but reflected back to them. This means that listening is far from passive. To let others know they're being heard involves body language that expresses your presence, like leaning toward them, making eye contact, and smiling with their happiness and wincing with their losses. To let others know they're being heard involves recapping what you hear from time to time and acknowledging with words as well as body language the feelings you feel they're having. These skills are at the heart of truly connecting with others. Listening in this way is powerful. People will remember how they felt when they were being listened to in this way long after they've forgotten the topic of conversation.

Mindful Disclosure

Any game of catch involves some skill in tossing as well as in catching. In the realm of interpersonal interactions, that means having some skill in disclosure as well as in listening. Gregory Kramer's recommendation to pause, relax, and open before speaking the truth is an extremely valuable approach for speaking from what's real and appropriate in any given interaction (Kramer 2008). When you speak from a place of being present, the person who is listening to you will also become more present. When you speak from a place of openheartedness and truth, it may resonate with others and call forth their own truth and openheartedness.

"Disclosing" is another type of "opening." In mindful disclosing, we open ourselves. This means moving in a direction opposite the self-enclosing pattern of problematic shyness and social anxiety. To practice disclosing, find someone with whom you feel it's safe to reveal yourself, then say how you really feel and ask for what you really want. Like mindful listening, mindful disclosing incorporates the attitudes of individual practice—being present without judging and without striving. This may require a strong intention to begin again and again, since judging comes up quite a bit for most of us—judging ourselves and judging those we're talking with. Staying in touch with your breath and the intention to be present without judging can help a lot. In fact, making it a practice to physically feel the breath periodically while in conversation with another person is one of the most effective ways you can cultivate mindfulness in interpersonal relationships.

Here are some important considerations in regard to mindful disclosing:

- Is what you are saying true?

- Is what you are saying beneficial?

- Could what you are saying hurt anybody?

- Are you striving in any way? For example, are you trying to meet someone else's expectations?

Nonstriving in self-disclosure involves letting go of any agenda you have to impress, please, control, or prove something to the person you are talking to and using all of the same skills as in mindful listening. The intention is to be open and trust that what you have to say will arise from what's most real in you. Of course, there are things that we want and don't want from one another, and there's nothing wrong with this. This is what human beings do. The invitation is to feel what you feel and do what you do with awareness and by making deliberate choices rather than reacting from unconscious habits. The intention is to notice when you feel these desires and aversions so that you might possess them and act on them consciously, deliberately, and with integrity rather than be possessed and driven by them.

To express what you want and need from another person involves disclosing yourself and asking for what you want without demanding or even expecting it. To express what you don't want from another person involves being specific and honest in what you're saying and being careful to neither express nor imply judgments. Conveying what you don't want is how you create boundaries and begins with the word "no." Expressing this artfully requires the skill of assertive communication.

Assertiveness

Assertiveness is expressing your thoughts, feelings, and desires directly in a way that's respectful and clear. It's neither aggressive nor passive, and it involves *I-statements*, as in "I want," "I feel," "I like," or "I don't like." If you can be skillful in saying no, you can teach others where you can and can't connect with them.

Here's a very useful formula for assertive communication:

1. When you [briefly describe a behavior],

2. I feel [an emotion]

3. because [briefly explain your way of perceiving this behavior].

4. What I want is [describe it briefly and specifically].

5. Will you [a very concrete, specific request]?

For example, you might express, "When you tell me how I should be driving, I feel offended and angry because that's what my dad used to do when he rode with me!" Pause. Does the other person understand your thoughts and feelings? If so, proceed to say something like "I would like it if you would talk with me about other things while I'm driving. I really do like talking with you when we're in the car, but I'm sensitive to backseat driving. Will you talk about something else unless we're genuinely in danger?"

distress tolerance

Psychologist Marsha Linehan, who created a therapeutic approach that combines cognitive behavioral techniques with mindfulness and acceptance, offers the term *distress tolerance* to describe one of the major skills in her approach, which is known as dialectical behavior therapy (Linehan 1993). Simply said, learning to tolerate distress—to maintain your center of balance in the midst of difficult thoughts and emotions—is vital to all interpersonal relationships. It's also one of the fruits of individual meditation practice.

In chapter 6, you explored distress tolerance with mindful yoga, mindfulness of uncomfortable sensations, and mindfulness of unpleasant emotions. Now you can begin to apply the same approach to interpersonal situations. In yoga practice, your muscles or joints may sometimes hurt. In sitting practice, your knees or back may ache and you're likely to experience unpleasant thoughts and emotions as mental content comes and goes. The spacious center you find inside yourself as you face and work with physical and emotional distress in these individual practices can help you a great deal as you face similar distressing thoughts and feelings in interpersonal relationships.

see for yourself exercise 7:
Situational Exposure

You can increase your ability to tolerate distress by exposure to social situations, both imagined and real, in which you feel anxious or uncomfortable (Henderson and Zimbardo 2001). Here's an outline of how the process works: First you come up with a list of social situations that are likely to elicit anxiety or shyness, and rate the severity of the anxiety, fear, or avoidance they're likely to provoke. Then you arrange the situations in a hierarchy from least to most distressing and begin to intentionally expose yourself to these situations to build tolerance, beginning with a low-ranked item. Now let's look at the process in detail.

Create a Hierarchy and Make a Plan

1. Take some time to consider the situations where you experience interpersonal anxiety and aversion. You can probably think of many, but you can also consult the list you created in chapter 7, in the exercise "Investigating Social

Aversion." You can include situations with just one person, with small groups, or with large groups of people. It will be helpful to create a list of situations that elicit feelings ranging from only mild distress to very intense distress.

2. Rank the intensity of your fear, anxiety, or avoidance for each situation using a scale of 0 to 100, where a rating of 0 means you don't avoid the situation or it doesn't provoke anxiety, and a rating of 100 means you always avoid the situation and it elicits panic or severe, continuous anxiety. If you hesitate to enter a situation but rarely avoid it, and it makes you slightly or somewhat anxious, assign it a rating between 20 and 40. If you sometimes avoid the situation and it definitely makes you anxious, assign it a rating between 40 and 60. If you usually avoid the situation and it makes you very anxious, assign it a rating between 60 and 80. Then arrange the items in a hierarchy, from least to most distressing. In case you find it helpful, here's a sample hierarchy (Henderson 2002):

95   Giving a presentation in front of thirty or more people

85   Asking someone I'm attracted to for a date

70   Agreeing to a date with someone I'm attracted to

65   Starting a conversation with a stranger of the opposite sex

60   Asking some colleagues from work out for lunch

55   Joining a group of others in conversation at work

50   Starting a conversation with a stranger of the same sex

40   Starting a conversation with a potential friend at work

35   Saying no to a request to help a colleague

30   Calling a friend from work to have a conversation

164

3. The next step is to plan your exposure practices, creating both a short-term and a long-term plan based on your hierarchy. Your short-term plan will involve the situations to turn toward in any given week, and your long-term plan will include the intentions you have for the months ahead. Your long-term goal is to become comfortable with as many of the items on your list as possible. Each week, you'll set a new short-term goal based what you achieved the previous week. For the first week, select one of the least challenging situations. It's a good idea to start with an item with a rating between 20 and 30. This ensures it's challenging enough to give you a sense of accomplishment without being too aversive.

Practice Exposure

1. Once you've selected a situation, begin to practice being in that situation. Start by practicing it in your imagination, and stay with it until your anxiety level decreases. Use the approach in the "Releasing Fear Meditation" in chapter 6 to help lower your anxiety level. This doesn't need to be an extreme reduction—a slight one will do. To be sure your anxiety has indeed diminished, assign it a rating before starting, using that same scale of 0 to 100. Try to stay in the imaginary situation until your anxiety level diminishes by at least 10 points. Know that this is difficult work. Acknowledge yourself for taking it on, and no matter how it turns out, reward yourself with your own congratulations and loving-kindness for taking on each practice.

2. Repeat the same practice frequently until your anxiety level decreases even more. It's a good idea to repeat the same practice or a variation on it every day until you experience less anxiety even as you enter the imagined situation.

3. If possible, ask a friend or family member to role-play the situation with you while you once again stay with it until your anxiety decreases.

4. The next step is to practice actually being in that situation in real life. Be sure to take the skills you've gained from

your imaginary and role-playing exposure with you into the situation. If you did engage in role-playing, it might be helpful to bring your role-playing partner along as a kind and supportive presence. Stay in touch with your breath and use your breath as an anchor to the present moment as often as possible in this practice.

5. Once you've overcome this first challenging situation, move up to the next item on your hierarchy.

It's important to actually schedule your exposure practices for each week so that you'll be sure to follow through on your intention to do this challenging work. As you progress through increasingly difficult situations over the next several weeks or months, you're likely to notice that your relationship to fear and anxiety is changing—that your way of looking at and responding to situations is less automatic and more flexible. The vicious habit of self-criticism can gradually recede as you discover more acceptance of what is. Remember that you aren't trying to get somewhere; you're practicing being in the here and now, accepting whatever distress arises and finding new ways to work with it. In time, you may find that you can create greater spaciousness in each successive practice and that fear doesn't have the same power to throw you into a trancelike state or into habits of avoidance and escape. As you engage in exposure practice, notice that you can make more and more space for mental, emotional, and sensory events of all kinds and that you can see them for what they are—impermanent experiences—not something to identify with, and not you, but just experiences.

Notes to Yourself

Take some time to write a bit about each exposure practice in your journal. You may notice that even writing about your experiences serves as another form of exposure and distress tolerance. Information to record might include date and duration of the exposure, a brief description of the situation you practiced (including whether you engaged in imaginary, role-playing, or real-life exposure), your anxiety level at the outset and at the end of each practice, and any thoughts and emotions you had about yourself, others, and the interaction.

mindfully online

Nowadays a huge amount of interpersonal relating happens in cyber-space through online mediums, and it's likely that our increasing reliance on social connection through e-mail, chat rooms, instant messaging, and the like has actually contributed to the growth in numbers of people who identify themselves as shy or suffering from social anxiety. A growing number of people earn their living entirely though cyberspace, and more and more people have come to rely on Internet resources to conduct much of the business of life, as well as personal relationships. Is it any wonder that, as a culture, we're developing more shyness and anxiety about interacting with others in person? In a world where technology is gradually taking the place of human touch, it's entirely possible to have most of our relationships happen online with people we seldom or never see.

Many teens report that they can be more themselves when chatting with friends online and are more accustomed to online communities than face-to-face encounters. MySpace, Facebook, my profile, my online friends—the list goes on, even to the point of creating entirely artificial cyberworlds in which we can assume avatars to represent us in virtual reality and interact with others who are visiting the same virtual places. Texting, the current craze, takes us even one step farther away from direct communication, replacing our previous addiction to talking constantly on cell phones. Amazingly, it's become so prevalent that it's been necessary to enact laws to prohibit texting while driving.

If any of this describes you, it might make sense to begin your interpersonal mindfulness practice online. It will certainly feel more natural to begin this work in a medium you feel familiar and somewhat comfortable with, and it may even be essential to begin these practices online if face-to-face encounters are extremely difficult for you. It is safer in some ways, because chatting online, exchanging e-mails, or joining an online community provides enough distance and space for many people to open up and share in ways that we rarely or never do in person. It can be easier to say things in writing rather than face-to-face, as evidenced in eloquent love letters that win the hearts of lovers and, sadly, in pathologically cruel hate letters that can break people's hearts.

Keeping all of these considerations in mind, you may find that, initially, you can become more centered and develop better communication

167

skills at the safe distance that Internet technologies provide. I've watched a lot of people who suffer with shyness grow in just this way as they've taken my mindfulness-based stress reduction classes online. In the first several weeks of classes many of these people have restricted their self-disclosures to the chat feature of our virtual classroom, but as they grow more mindful and capable of maintaining a sense of personal balance while communicating, they "graduate" to using their microphones and eventually even their webcams to connect with the rest of the class. You could consider a similar approach to eventually meeting an online friend face-to-face. The intention is to use technology to increase your interpersonal mindfulness skills so that you can eventually better connect and attune yourself with others in person.

It's important to understand that the same distance that makes Internet communications a little safer also interferes with the intimacy and resonance that actually being with others provides. We exchange a huge amount of energy with one another when we're in each other's physical presence, and this can't be replicated online. Bodies communicate with one another in ways we are just beginning to recognize with the sophisticated instruments of neurobiology. For example, we now know that human beings have mirror neurons in their brains that can align with the emotional states of the people we're with. When we're in close proximity to one another, the neurological activities of one person's brain can attune with those of another person, as indicated by studies of mothers with their infants and counselors with their clients (Schore 2003). In addition, there are a great many ways we communicate nonverbally through sometimes minute variations in posture, gait, gestures, and facial expressions, as well as pheromones, which communicate many things, including sexual availability, hostility, and fear, through our sense of smell. Many of these forms of communication aren't possible in cyberspace, even when we use webcams.

If you think you might like to begin your mindfulness practice online, see the Resources section for information on MBSR online programs and other Internet resources. If you're interested in cultivating a formal interpersonal mindfulness practice online, consider exploring the resources available at Gregory Kramer's website, www.metta.org or at www.minfullivingprograms.com.

schedule practice

Please take a moment now to schedule daily mindfulness practice with the exercises exploring insight dialogue and other practices from this book. Also be sure to schedule your practice of exposure to challenging social situations. If you are using the MPTS Program and workbook, this is the time for you to begin Insight Dialog practice with others.

a calling to remember

Even if you feel painfully shy, it's important to know that you have internal resources for empathy and connectedness with others that you can cultivate with mindfulness practices. As in all things, whether physical exercise, playing the piano, or painting with watercolors, the time you spend in practice is beneficial. You grow more skillful with every hour and minute you invest. As you spend more time cultivating mindfulness in interpersonal relationships, you can discover and begin to dissolve obstacles like unrealistic desires and fears. As you free yourself from these old, imprisoning habits of mind, you can finally meet others in the here and now with far less clutter and noise in your mind.

Meeting others in this way opens the door to attunement and resonance, which in turn give rise to the spirit of compassion and loving-kindness. Compassion and loving-kindness, the subject of the next chapter, are their own rewards.

the healing power
of compassion

9

A human being is part of a whole called by us universe, a part limited in time and space. We experience ourselves, our thoughts and feelings, as something separate from the rest—a kind of optical delusion of consciousness. This delusion is a kind of prison for us, restricting us to our personal desires and to affection for a few persons nearest us. Our task must be to free ourselves from this prison by widening our circle of compassion to embrace all living creatures and the whole of nature in its beauty.

—Albert Einstein

Everyone can benefit by taking Einstein's beautiful words to heart, as they reveal not only how we imprison ourselves with delusions of separateness, but also how we may free ourselves from this prison. This is the pathway of compassion and loving-kindness, and following it can free you from the private self-consciousness of shyness and social anxiety.

Each moment you invest in mindfulness practice can quiet a little more of the noise in your head and enable you to find a place to rest in your own deep being. The more you can be at home in your own deep being, the more you may discover the ways you're connected with everyone and everything else. It's not that our many differences don't exist; they obviously and often tragically do. We are a world of conflicting nationalities, religions, races, and cultures. Even within our warring nations, we separate ourselves from one another with different political parties and beliefs about everything from sports teams to God, creating wounds that only serve to further separate us from one another. It's not that mindfulness can erase these differences; in fact, it may make them more vivid. It's that mindfulness reveals the many ways we are part of a larger whole—a whole that we may learn to serve by embodying acceptance and compassion as a way of life.

When you bring this awareness into interpersonal mindfulness practice, you can witness how the circles of compassion grow larger and unite you with others. You can see and feel the ways in which no one wants to feel frightened or alone, and that no one wants to suffer. In interpersonal mindfulness practice, you can have the immediate experience of being an individual, separate in your own body and skin, and simultaneously recognize the ways you are deeply connected with others. You can see that you are just as much a part of "we" as you are a "me." One of the gifts of interpersonal mindfulness practice is having the experience of knowing and being known by others in this place of the heart, where we are all connected. The walls of your self-constructed prison crumble and fall away as you grow in openhearted awareness and extend more acceptance and compassion to yourself and others.

It's interesting that the word "alone" is a composite of two words, "all one." If you explore some of the deep meanings of this word, you discover that it's characterized by concepts like "unity" and "undivided." From this context, being alone is quite different from being isolated. Like an ostrich with its head in the sand, we may choose to isolate ourselves in a private self-consciousness, but we can never succeed in actually separating ourselves from everyone else.

the way of transformation

Many years ago I bought a piece of land that was covered with the invasive weed star thistle. At least five acres of the land was infested with this sharp and unfriendly weed that crowded out most other plants. I visited a friend who's an organic farmer to ask his advice. It was simple: "Discourage what you don't want and encourage what you do want."

I bought an antique tractor with a huge mower and mowed the entire field before anything could flower and create more seed. I did this three times over a few months and then waited for the spring rains. When the rains came, the biggest work began. I started scattering seeds of native grasses and other plants. That summer I mowed the field again, and when the rains came again I redoubled my seed sowing. The next year I mowed the field only once and then let all the plants I had sown go to seed before mowing again to scatter that seed everywhere. Every year the field changed as the new plants grew and multiplied and, gradually over a few years, the star thistle mostly disappeared and a lovely field of grass and wildflowers appeared.

Many years have passed, and I as I look over that field today I can see that it now does a great job of taking care of itself, requiring no outside assistance to remain healthy and manage its own weed problems. It still hosts some star thistle but is by no means defined by it. It's using a capacity for self-regulation and self-healing that was always there but needed a little help after years of being abused by excessive grazing of the grasses.

Freeing yourself from the pain and suffering of shyness is similar. You need to do a little to discourage the weeds of self-blame and fear, and you need to do a lot to sow and cultivate compassion and loving-kindness. The intention is to put a lot more energy into what you want rather than struggling with what you don't want. You can be generous in sowing the seeds of compassion in the field of your awareness by practicing loving-kindness meditation every day.

compassion is the key that sets you free

Compassion can grow as you turn toward those dark and sometimes despised and neglected parts of your own consciousness that you usually try to ignore or dispel. You may find compassion in the wounds of your own self-blame, self-hate, and shame. You may find it in a cherished victimhood. Compassion is the small door that's wide open in a dark corner of your self-constructed prison cell, a way out that you'll never notice as long as you're intent on avoiding ugly, scary places inside of yourself.

My friend Beth Roth, a well-known mindfulness teacher, once said that compassion is a special kind of love that arises to meet the pain of suffering. With time and practice, you may grow in your ability to attune to other people and learn to empathize with their emotions because you've learned to respond with kindness to the emotions in your own heart.

Everyone has to cope with loss and fear and sorrow. Look for these feelings in others from time to time and allow your own heart to open and respond to them with loving-kindness. "Compassion" literally means "to suffer with," and also to care for and wish to alleviate another person's suffering. When you encounter someone else's sorrow or fear, remember the elements of Gregory Kramer's insight dialogue practice: pause, relax, open, and trust emergence. Something will arise in your heart to respond to the other person's heart and connect the two of you in ways that are mutually beneficial.

When you extend loving-kindness to others, it's somewhat like offering a fragrant flower to a friend; some of the fragrance lingers on your hand. We know this in our hearts and can now measure it in neuroimaging studies. The research conducted by Richard Davidson (Davidson et al. 2003; Davidson 2006), discussed in chapter 2, demonstrates the profound individual benefit of practicing loving-kindness and compassion. By extending our very best and warmest wishes to others, we can't help but create these mental and emotional states in ourselves, and these benefits can be measured by changes that occur in the brain. As Daniel Goleman notes in his book *Destructive Emotions* (2003), we ourselves are the most immediate beneficiaries of the compassion we extend to all others.

• Discoveries on the Path: *A Chimpanzee's Story*

Jack Kornfield told a story about the connections we form through compassion at a conference I attended in 2007. A woman psychologist was walking across the campus at Berkeley and came upon a large group of men gathered around a couple of chimpanzees, one on a leash and the other free. As she stopped to see what was happening, the woman recognized that the chimp on the leash was a female who had been brought to help capture the male, who was free.

Obviously the effort had been successful. The male had a hold on the female's leash and was trying to pull her to mate with him. The female was just as obviously not into this and was trying to pull away. Some of the men who were watching were encouraging the male, and the female's handler evidently wasn't trying to help her. The woman psychologist's heart was immediately filled with compassion for the female chimp.

At just that moment, the female chimp turned to her and made eye contact, then yanked her leash away from the male chimp and her handler and walked directly over and took the woman's hand. They both stood looking at the now silent group of men. Then the female chimp saw or felt another woman at the other edge of this group and led the woman psychologist over to her and took her hand as well. As they stood there silently but deeply connected, the men dispersed and the handlers quietly took charge of their chimps.

Compassion is more powerful than we may think. Just by feeling it we send unseen messages to other people and other creatures. Just by opening our hearts to compassion, we may be able to help and be helped by each other in ways we don't fully know or understand. Every single human being needs such help. We heal ourselves and one another with this kind support.

The Value of Kind Support

It's not just painful encounters and humiliating experiences that can lock you into an anxious prison of shyness, it's how you and those closest to you respond to the hurt and humiliation you feel. How you deal with hurt, guilt, and fear can make the difference between growing more shy or less shy.

For example, the research of Jerome Kagan (1994) shows that parents can help their children with shyness a great deal by providing them with a secure base that's safe and can be counted on in times of fear or anxiety. If children feel connected to their parents and receive compassionate support from that connection, they can go out into the world and take on scary challenges again and again and reduce their anxiety a bit with each experience, even if a challenging experience is painful and doesn't work out well. What's important is the consistent kind and loving support. If their parents are there for them, children can learn resiliency and develop a sense of personal agency—a sense that they can accomplish desired outcomes on their own behalf. The ability to cope with shyness has a lot to do with how we are cared for and learn to care for ourselves when we are hurting.

We tend to maintain the personality traits we learned as children. Though we dwell in a grown-up body, on the inside many of us are still the frightened little kid we were so many years ago. And even if we do outgrow our fears and self-doubts, no one outgrows the need for love and compassion. Some of us may have to learn how to give ourselves the safe and secure base of self-compassion that we never had before. We can do this through our own self-compassion and loving-kindness.

Self-Compassion

A painful habit of people who feel shy and socially anxious is reviewing personal collections of negative self-beliefs and judgments. Not only is this no fun, you can become so consumed with your thoughts, feelings, appearance, and behavior that you have a difficult time understanding, empathizing with, or even noticing anyone else. Usually the phrase "full of himself" refers to someone who is exhibitionistic or vain, but in truth, we're just as full of ourselves when we're under the spell of negative self-talk. This is how we create the state of mind that makes us feel separate from the fundamental essence of life that we share with all others.

As a state of mind, shyness is maintained thoughts and behaviors that, to go back to the quote from Einstein that opened this chapter, are "restricting us to our personal desires" by creating an "optical delusion of consciousness" (1996, pp. 10-11). It's a prison of ideas. When in this state of mind, you experience yourself as separate from everyone else and create a prison for yourself, maintained and guarded by a scared internal gatekeeper who tells you things like "I've been wronged and taken advantage of," "Don't trust them," or "They can tell there's something wrong with me." Einstein suggested that we must "free ourselves from this prison by widening our circle of compassion to embrace all living creatures" (p. 11). Remember that you too are a living creature, and in fact, your compassion for others needs to start with compassion for yourself, just like the heart infuses itself with blood before sending it to the rest of your body.

At a conference I attended in 2007, professor Kristin Neff, Ph.D., of the University of Texas in Austin, illuminated some important differences between the concepts "self-esteem" and "self-compassion" that changed my way of thinking about self-esteem. As it turns out, the concept of self-esteem can actually create more problems than benefits. For example, if you come to the conclusion that your self-esteem is poor, you may go to work on trying to improve it but, in the end, rarely if ever feel like you're good enough. That's because no one is quite certain how much self-esteem is enough, though everyone seems to know what too little is. Many people who identify as being shy say they have low self-esteem even though they've been trying to improve it for years on end. Maybe it would be worthwhile to just discard the whole self-esteem concept and replace it with self-compassion. After all, no matter what your level of self-esteem, you can always extend compassion to yourself.

Self-compassion doesn't mean pitying or feeling sorry for yourself, nor is it even empathy, as all of these responses to suffering are one step removed from suffering. Compassion is the loving-kindness that responds to suffering like a loving mother turns toward her crying baby. Not only is there a deep inquiry into what's wrong, there's also a caring response concerned with alleviating the suffering. Such self-compassion is one of the greatest gifts you could ever give to yourself, and it will carry you through the most difficult of challenges when nothing else seems to help.

Sometimes you might need to jump-start your self-compassion by beginning with others. One way is to look for people who seem shy and see if you can see the same fearfulness or hurt in their eyes and faces that you know in your own heart. You'll probably have to look closely to find this, as most people put up a good front. Extend your empathy and compassion for the unhappiness you witness in others, and let your heart go out to the suffering and loneliness you experience in their eyes. By giving compassion to others, you may learn how to give it to yourself also.

When you find a spark of self-compassion, nurture it and encourage its growth. Practicing self-compassion daily can heal your aching heart, and even your body, at the deepest levels. It is a noble endeavor that can greatly assist you in finding your way through shyness.

Compassion in Action

In the words of the Roman philosopher and statesman Seneca, "If you wish to be loved, love" (1969, p. 49). This includes extending compassion to yourself. As you learned in chapter 7, loving-kindness is an expression of compassion that you first give to yourself. From there it may spread out to others—everyone from loved ones to adversaries, and eventually to all living beings. Whenever you find yourself repeating familiar judgments about what's wrong with you (I'm so stupid, bad, worthless, pathetic, whatever), extend expressions of loving-kindness to yourself. These are the moments when you most need your own compassion. Offer yourself these kind words, which I learned from my dear friend Howard Blumenfeld: "May I awaken to my loving heart and follow its path of compassion and wisdom."

Your compassion and loving-kindness will grow just like ripples on a pond. One small word or act of compassion can go quite far. It starts inside your own mind, as you extend whatever compassion you can to yourself. This enables you to shift out of your habitual thinking patterns and fear-laden self-talk a bit. In this moment, you are no longer mired in self-blame and can be suffused with self-compassion. As the self-judgments quiet down, you can discover a larger well of compassionate awareness within that can extend to others quite naturally.

I recently attended a meeting with Jon Kabat-Zinn and eighty other MBSR teachers and was deeply moved to hear the many ways these wonderful teachers extend compassion in their lifework. As I began my long drive home, I stopped to ask a taxi driver for directions to the freeway. I watched as he gently helped his frail, elderly passenger from the car, hoisted up all of her packages, and then took her arm in a long journey of tiny steps to the building. He stopped a few times so she could rest and once so she could talk with a friend. He nearly carried her up the stairs. Watching him brought tears to my eyes as his patience, tenderness, and compassion touched my heart.

I tried to express my appreciation of what he had done, but even though he had spent at least fifteen minutes helping his passenger, he wouldn't accept my acknowledgment. He told me that this is what we all must do for one another—that giving to those who need is how he lives his life, and how he hopes everyone might live. As he pointed me on my way to the freeway and turned back to his taxi, I bowed to him in gratitude anyway.

Though this was just a single incident encountered along the way, it goes to show that we can embody compassion in whatever work is given to us. As your compassion grows, little by little you may surrender more of the habits of mind that separate you from others and discover the wonder and beauty of the people around you. You'll discover that the compassion you extend to other beings mirrors the compassion you offer to yourself.

Sometimes it's easiest to begin extending compassion to others by first offering it to someone you love as a loving-kindness meditation. Acknowledge to yourself whatever pain or suffering you know this person has endured. If you want, imagine you're holding this person in some way, and let your own heart feel this person's hurt. Then offer your most sincere wishes for freedom from pain and suffering:

I care for this frightened and unhappy heart.
May you be free from suffering.
May you be at peace and know ease of being.
May you be happy in this life just as it is.

With time, you can extend this compassion for a loved one to "embrace all living creatures and the whole of nature in its beauty" (Einstein 1996, p. 11). The moment your heart joins with another's, you are no longer alone and separate. From this small beginning, the circle spreads outward. Just like waves that can cross oceans and touch many shores, the compassion you find in your own heart may in time connect you with everyone else and wash away the suffering of shyness and social anxiety. As Jack Kornfield has observed, "The things that matter most in our lives aren't fantastic or grand. They are the moments when we touch one another" (1993, p. 14).

see for yourself exercise 8:
Practicing Compassion Informally

Each day for the next week, find some time to invest yourself in extending compassion and loving-kindness to the people around you. For example, if you're standing in line, look around and see if you can open your heart to others who are standing nearby. They may be speaking in different languages or have very different clothing than you do. See if you can find the right words to invite them into your heart, like "These are my brothers and sisters" or "We're all in this together." See if you can pick up on the feelings of the people around you and find some resonance with the feelings you have in your own heart. Extend your best and warmest wishes to those around you, using some of the phrases from your loving-kindness practice if you like. You may be sending these wishes to the back of the person's head, yet sometimes people pick up on good intentions from afar and will turn to look at you. If you feel like it and it seems safe, smile to express the feelings you have in your heart. You may be surprised to discover that the person smiles back.

Please use your best discretion as you invest yourself in this practice. You might start by simply paying the toll for the driver behind you or by extending your heartfelt compassion to people who are suffering from illness or in war-torn places. Let it grow.

Notes to Yourself

Take some time to contemplate your experiences practicing compassion, then write about this in your journal.

the power of forgiveness

We can't avoid judgments and resentments, toward others and toward ourselves. They are a part of human nature. What we can do is acknowledge these feelings as they come up and forgive ourselves and others. Like the fabled philosopher's stone in alchemy, forgiveness can transmute the baseness of blame and resentment into the gold of love. However, it doesn't mean minimizing your hurt; in fact, it's the opposite. Before you can heal from emotional injuries or begin to forgive, you have to allow yourself to feel your feelings completely, perhaps more deeply then ever before. Look for the truth, feeling into emotions, acknowledging, and letting be.

Sometimes forgiving is a large part of compassion. Forgiving is "for giving" to yourself, and you'll find that it's a medicine that heals at the deepest levels. Forgiveness is often what we need to give ourselves above all other things. Self-forgiveness is an intention and practice, and like any other practice it starts with what you can do or offer, even if it's quite small. Sometimes it may seem as though you're just mouthing the words, but these words are essential. You need self-forgiveness because there's a good chance that you are your own worst enemy. Forgiveness may allow you to lay your burden down and quit carrying the heavy load of self-blame.

Exercise:
Preparing to Forgive

You may blame yourself habitually for all manner of things, large and small. Sometimes these accusations aren't even true, and yet you may have repeated them for years. Over the next week, notice all the ways you blame yourself, and record them in your journal. The things on your list might be judgments about yourself (your appearance, intelligence, and so on) or about your actions with others. At the end of the week, rate these thoughts on a scale of 0 to 10, with 10 being the most difficult and painful, then use the following procedure as you start with the least difficult thing on your list:

1. Consider something you've been blaming yourself for. Hold it in your awareness and examine it as a physician would look into a wound to see what may be lodged there that's preventing it from healing. With curiosity, nonjudgment, and patience, look into it again and again from every angle.

2. Truly feel the hurt and anger attached to this self-blame as deeply as you can. Understand that it's important to know your hurt and feel at its core if you are ever to release it. Feel the weight of this hurt and hold it with openhearted awareness.

3. I learned from Jon Kabat-Zinn that the word "suffer" has its origins in a Latin word that mean "to carry." Imagine how you would feel if you were no longer angry at yourself and blaming yourself. Imagine what it would be like to set this burden down.

4. Understand that forgiveness isn't about changing the past or anything about yourself or anyone else. It's about making new beginnings, and sometimes it's about making amends. It's about laying a burden down. Consider if you need to make amends to yourself or to others for this burden of blame you've been carrying. Be certain that whatever amends you choose to make cause no further harm.

5. Commit to taking the actions you feel are called for.

6. If you want, apply this same process to the burden of blame you carry about someone else, again starting with the least painful item on a list. See if you can form the intention to forgive this person. Just hold that intention, going no further for now, particularly if this person has caused you grievous harm. If at any time it feels right to you and you feel ready, you can return to this intention to see if you can go a little further, waiting and watching for a release of blame or hatred just as you wait for a release of tension in mindful yoga practice. One day, you may be ready to offer this person some measure of forgiveness in the same way you've offered forgiveness to yourself.

mindfulness practice:
Forgiveness

Know that forgiveness is a gift of love and compassion that you must first extend to yourself. In this practice, you'll offer forgiveness to yourself for self-injury, forgiveness to yourself for injuring others, and forgiveness to others for injuring you. Please note one important point before you begin: If you're working with a serious life trauma, be sensitive to your needs. You may wish to seek support from a counselor or trusted friend as you undertake this practice. And remember: If someone has hurt you or abused you, forgiving does not mean that what happened was okay or that you want to reconcile. If someone is hurting or abusing you now, this practice is not meant to enable further abuse; rather, use it to help you care for yourself as you seek help to end the abuse. Forgiveness practice enables you to stop carrying painful and poisonous memories and feelings around with you and is a way to strip others' power to hurt you by means of the blame and hatred you've carried in your own mind.

To begin, practice mindfulness of the breath for at least ten minutes. As you near the end of your breathing practice, concentrate your attention into the vicinity of your chest and feel your breath coming and going there. Feel deeply into your chest and see if you can sense the beating of your heart. Notice if your chest or heart responds in some way to your friendly attention. Then offer yourself and others these words of forgiveness, repeating them as many times as you need to:

I forgive myself for the injuries I have caused myself, both knowingly and unknowingly, through ignorance, greed, fear, and anger.
May I be free from mental and physical suffering.
May I be at peace.
May I be happy.

I forgive myself for the injuries I have caused others, both knowingly and unknowingly, through ignorance, greed, fear, and anger.
May I be free from mental and physical suffering.
May I be at peace.
May I be happy.

I forgive you for the injuries you have caused me, both knowingly and unknowingly, through ignorance, greed, fear, and anger.
May you be free from mental and physical suffering.
May you be at peace.
May you be happy.

Afterward, sit for a few minutes and practice mindfulness of the breath; then, when you're ready, thank yourself for this gift of forgiveness.

Notes to Yourself

Forgiveness is a powerful practice that, like meditation itself, is not for the faint of heart. Notice what came up for you in these practices: what you resisted and struggled with, what old wounds surfaced, what unfinished business you still carry around long after a painful event, and what happened in your body as you investigated these experiences. Then take some time to write in your journal about your experiences with practicing forgiveness.

healing as an internal resource

Some of the work of meditation is looking inward and exploring the difficult and dark territory of painful thoughts and feelings that you've probably tried to avoid for much of your life. Mindfulness will bring light into these dark places.

If you identify as shy, you're probably all too familiar with a cruel internal critic. You may wonder if you could ever be compassionate with yourself after so many years of self-blame and self-punishment. Know that the capacity for self-compassion lies within you, even if you don't know where it is yet. In your physical body, compassion is expressed in the mechanism of analgesia so many of us have experienced at the time of a serious injury, wherein we don't suffer as much pain as it seems the injury should cause. At the time of this writing I injured my finger (it was bent sideways!), yet for the first twenty-four hours I felt very little pain. We have internal resources of mercy that can sometimes protect us from physical pain that's too great to bear.

In the realm of the mind, a similar mechanism is *disassociation*, an automatic mental process that protects you from being overwhelmed by traumatic experiences. In the midst of a terrible trauma, disassociation enables a shift into a consciousness that seems to be witnessing what's happening from a short distance away, as if you've become a dispassionate spectator. You see and experience what's happening, but mercifully you don't feel it.

You don't have to know how to do these things. Healing arises from a source inside of you that knows how to heal you. If you accidentally bang your shin on the table, you don't have to figure out how to mend your leg; your body begins to help itself immediately by sending legions of healing forces, along with blood and swelling, to the site of injury. It cares for itself. In time the pain subsides and the swelling and bruising disappear.

Your mind knows how to care for itself in similar ways. When you ran into the table, you may have felt a wave of anger sweep over you for hitting the same table with the same shin for the umpteenth time. You might have some choice words for yourself, but in a little while the anger subsides. The mind eventually soothes itself, and you come back into an emotional steady state. In terms of shyness and social anxiety, an overanxious mind also wants to return to its steady state, and at some level it knows how to do so. Like the whole of nature, your body and mind possess a natural homeostasis that knows how to balance and heal you.

It's fortunate that you don't have to figure out how to heal your own body by consciously commandeering forces of white corpuscles, blood clotting agents, or any of the other body's miracles of self-defense. None of us is smart enough to do that. What you can do is try to reduce inflammation and promote the healing your body will naturally provide. You can also start paying better attention as you pass by that table. In that sense, your anger at yourself for walking into the table might help you not run into the table again.

Similarly, you don't need to figure out how to balance and heal your mind. It also has natural capacities for self-healing. You don't have to learn how to send self-soothing neurotransmitters to calm your inflamed amygdala. Most of us don't even know what or where the amygdala is, let alone how to calm it down!

But there are times when your mind and body can fall into dysregulation and be unable to return to homeostasis. This is what happened to the field that was covered with star thistle, mentioned earlier in this chapter. At these times, mindfulness can help you reclaim your balance and promote the healing powers that reside within you. For example, you can become aware of self-blaming and shaming thoughts and look deeply into them. Are they true? Are they necessary? When you find these thoughts, you may choose to quit encouraging them with so much of your attention. For example, you might practice forgiveness rather than self-blame. Like grasses and wildflowers that replace noxious weeds when the rains come, compassion arises when given a place and a chance to grow. As loving-kindness and compassion become strong in you, the noxious thoughts and fears that have separated you from others will fade away.

schedule practice

Please take a moment now to schedule these forgiveness and compassion practices into the coming week. It will continue to serve you best to practice every day, perhaps interspersing these practices with others you've learned in this book or developed on your own.

a calling to remember

Perhaps there are few better ways to describe shyness and social anxiety than as a prison in which people experience themselves and their thoughts and feelings as something separate from others—as Einstein said, "a kind of optical delusion of consciousness" (1996, p. 10). I believe there's no better way to free yourself from this prison than with the compassion you find in your own heart and can share with others.

epilogue:
a hidden wholeness

Life has no other discipline to impose, if we would but realize it, than to accept life unquestioningly. Everything we shut our eyes to, everything we run away from, everything we deny, denigrate, or despise, serves to defeat us in the end. What seems nasty, painful, evil, can become a source of beauty, joy, and strength, if faced with an open mind. Every moment is a golden one for him who has the vision to recognize it as such.

—Henry Miller

Practicing meditation is like opening up a space in your mind where you can witness everything that arises in your thoughts, emotions, and sensations—everything. In this space you become aware of life as it is, independent of your preferences. You see the past as it is and see that it cannot be changed. You see yourself as you are and everything and everyone around you as they are, and you know that no one and nothing can escape change. As you peer into this space, you see those things that you desire and those that you despise. You also see that it doesn't really matter to life if you desire or despise anything; it's going to serve up just what it's going to serve up, and you must ultimately find a way to accept what that is in each moment.

In time you may see that, in this unconditional acceptance and spaciousness of mind, there is a source of joy, beauty, and strength that could not be known as long as you were struggling and striving for something else. As you let go of desires, attachments, judgments, and complaints, you come home to the simple delight of being alive, and being whole just as you are in this moment.

Think of your mindfulness as a mirror—a totally receptive space that's open and accepting of all things, a spaciousness that may be filled or emptied without judgment, clinging, or resistance. Much of the work we've done together in this book has been to help you cultivate this wide-open awareness—a place from which you can experience yourself and everyone else as sharing in the ongoing, unfolding experience of life. From this point of view, you may come to know that the critical and striving parts of your personality are what have made you feel separate from others, and that far from being alone, you are deeply connected through life itself to everyone else. This is an important discovery, and the more you feel this depth of connection, the more you can free yourself from the painful isolation of shyness and social anxiety.

Every human being will always have room for many kinds of improvements; we're all imperfect. The recognition of your fundamental wholeness doesn't change this simple fact, but it does allow you to accept that there will always be something about you that is imperfect. Even as you continue to engage in living your life to the fullest, to be all that you may be, you can find a center within yourself that is fundamentally sufficient and good enough, just as it is. This is a good place to operate from as you attend to all of the responsibilities of being human. From the wide-open space of mindfulness and acceptance, you can discover that life is vibrant with great beauty, joy, and freedom, just as it is.

Some years ago I worked with a client who discovered his wholeness only after a trip to Mexico, during which he visited an archeological site where an ancient temple was being hacked out of the jungle. When he returned to therapy after his trip, he was visibly lighter and happier. He told me that he had finally realized this one, precious fruit of mindfulness: that some part of him was very much like that temple—perfect, whole, and complete, needing no improvement whatsoever—and that it was simply overgrown with a veritable jungle of concepts and ideas of self, mostly formed of judgments and assumptions that had obscured who he really was.

where to go from here?

Really, there is no other place to go but here, and no time to be but now. On the mindful path, here is the beginning point and the destination, and the journey is always beginning again now. That said, sometimes it is helpful to take a literal journey to more deeply experience the here and the now. There are many places where you can go to further and deepen your practice: retreat centers for extended meditation practice with experienced mindfulness teachers, weekend meditation groups, and more. You may be able to find a group of people in your community practicing mindfulness meditation (also called insight meditation or vipassana meditation) together on weekly basis. Know that it's extremely helpful and beneficial to meditate with others. Although each of us is responsible for our own practice, that doesn't mean you have to go it alone. There are ways in which we can practice and support one another in meditation together. It's good to sit with others in weekly practice groups or in retreat settings, where you can deeply invest yourself in meditation practice.

Although you've come to the end of this book, your journey with mindfulness continues. Please consult the Resources section for information on how to find meditation groups in your area. You'll also find a list of online resources that can provide you access to a wider community of people who are invested in mindfulness, as well as further instruction in meditation via online programs. In addition, you'll find some information on audio and video resources that can benefit you in your meditation practice. Use whatever resources seem right to you to further your practice. Most importantly, continue to create a daily practice and a special place in your home for meditation. Begin again and again and again.

It is my deepest wish that you discover the wholeness within you, and through it realize peace, joy, and ease of being in your relationships with others. May your heart be filled with loving-kindness. May you be happy. May you be at peace. May all beings be at peace.

> How did the rose ever open its heart
> And give to this world all its beauty?
> It felt the encouragement of light against its being.
> Otherwise, we all remain too frightened.
>
> —Hafiz

resources

recommended reading

Antony, M. M., and R. P. Swinson. 2008. *The Shyness and Social Anxiety Workbook.* 2nd ed. Oakland, CA: New Harbinger.

Benett-Goleman, T. 2001. *Emotional Alchemy: How the Mind Can Heal the Heart.* New York: Harmony Books.

Biegel, G. 2010. *The Stress Reduction Workbook for Teens: Mindfulness Skills to Help You Deal with Stress.* Oakland, CA: New Harbinger Publications.

Bieling, P. J., and M. M. Antony. 2000. *The Shyness and Social Anxiety Workbook.* Oakland, CA: New Harbinger.

Bourne, E. 2000. *The Anxiety and Phobia Workbook.* Oakland, CA: New Harbinger.

Chödrön, P. 2001. *The Places That Scare You.* Boston: Shambhala.

Epstein, M. 1995. *Thoughts Without a Thinker: Psychotherapy from a Buddhist Perspective.* New York: Basic Books.

Goldstein, J. 1987. *Being Peace.* Berkeley, CA: Parallax Press.

Goldstein, J. 1993. *Insight Meditation.* Boston: Shambhala.

Goldstein, J., and J. Kornfield. 2001. *Seeking the Heart of Wisdom.* Boston: Shambhala.

Hayes, S. C., with S. Smith. 2005. *Get Out of Your Mind and Into Your Life: The New Acceptance and Commitment Therapy.* Oakland, CA: New Harbinger.

Kabat-Zinn, J. 1990. *Full Catastrophe Living: Using the Wisdom of Your Body and Mind to Face Stress, Pain, and Illness.* New York: Delacorte Press.

Kabat-Zinn, J. 1994. *Wherever You Go, There You Are: Mindfulness Meditation in Everyday Life.* New York: Hyperion.

Kabat-Zinn, J. 2005. *Coming to Our Senses: Healing Ourselves and the World Through Mindfulness.* New York: Hyperion.

Kornfield, J. 2003. *The Art of Forgiveness, Lovingkindness, and Peace.* New York: Bantam Books.

Kornfield, J. 2008. *The Wise Heart: A Guide to the Universal Teachings of Buddhist Psychology.* New York: Random House.

McKay, M., M. David, and P. Fanning. 1995. *Messages: The Communications Skills Workbook.* Oakland, CA: New Harbinger.

Nhat Hanh, T. 1999. *The Miracle of Mindfulness: A Manual on Meditation.* Boston: Beacon Press.

Rosenberg, L., with D. Guy. 1998. *Breath by Breath: The Liberating Practice of Insight Meditation.* Boston: Shambhala.

Salzberg, S. 1995. *Loving-Kindness: The Revolutionary Art of Happiness.* Boston: Shambhala.

Salzberg, S. 1997. *A Heart as Wide as the World.* Boston: Shambhala.

Santorelli, S. 1999. *Heal Thyself.* New York: Bell Tower.

Stahl, B. and E. Goldstein. 2010. *A Mindfulness-Based Stress Reduction Workbook.* Oakland, CA: New Harbinger Publications.

Tolle, E. 2003. *Stillness Speaks.* Vancouver, BC: Namaste Publishing.

Tolle, E. 2005. *A New Earth.* New York: Dutton.

Welwood, J. 1996. *Love and Awakening: Discovering the Sacred Path of Intimate Relationship.* San Francisco: Harper Collins.

meditation recordings

To purchase audio recordings of the body scan and other guided mindfulness practices, visit the website of Mindful Living Programs (www.

mindfullivingprograms.com) or Awareness and Relaxation Training (www.mindfulnessprograms.com).

meditation retreats and retreat centers

Mindful Living Programs: www.mindfullivingprograms.com. Retreats, including accredited continuing education retreats for medical and mental health professions, are offered at several locations in California.

Awareness and Relaxation Training: www.mindfulnessprograms.com. Retreats are offered in Santa Cruz, California.

Insight Meditation Society, located in Barre, Massachusetts: 978-355-4378; www.dharma.org/ims.

Spirit Rock Meditation Center, located in Woodacre, California: 415-488-0164; www.spiritrock.org.

Gaia House, located in West Ogwell, Newton Abbot, Devon, England: 44-0-1626-333613; www.gaiahouse.co.uk.

mindfulness-based stress reduction programs

To locate mindfulness-based stress reduction (MBSR), consult the resources below, or search the Internet for "MBSR" or "mindfulness-based stress reduction."

University of Massachusetts Medical Center: 55 Lake Avenue North, Worcester, MA 01655; 508-856-2656; www.umassmed.edu/cfm/index.aspx. MBSR was developed at the University of Massachusetts Medical Center. Use the website listed here to locate MBSR programs internationally.

Online MBSR programs: www.mindfullivingprograms.com. I've created an online MBSR program, which takes place live, in real time, using state-of-the-art video conferencing software.

Enloe Medical Center: 1531 Esplanade, Chico, California, 95926; 530-332-6724. I'm the director of the MBSR program here. You can contact me directly at steve@mindfullivingprograms.com.

internet social anxiety and mindfulness resources

www.mindfullivingprograms.com. At this site you may download the Mindful Path Through Shyness Program and workbook.

www.aliveworld.com/shops/mh1/Mindfulness_2C00_-Anxiety-and-Stress.aspx

www.acceptanceandmindfulness.com

www.act-for-anxiety-disorders.com

shyness resources

The Shyness Institute: www.shyness.com.

American Psychological Association shyness page: www.apa.org/topics/topicshyness.html.

finding a therapist

For Shyness and Anxiety

County or state mental health agencies or psychology boards. Call and ask for referrals to therapists who specialize in treatment of shyness or anxiety.

American Psychological Association. 800-964-2000. Ask for referrals to therapists who specialize in treatment of shyness.

Anxiety Disorders Association of America. 240-485-1001; www.adaa.org.

California Association of Marriage and Family Therapists. 858-292-2638; www.camft.org. Ask for referrals to therapists who specialize in treatment of shyness.

Social Anxiety Association. www.socialphobia.org.

Therapists Specializing in ACT, DBT, MBCT, and Mindfulness-Based Approaches

Association for Contextual Behavioral Science. www.contextualpsycho logy.org/therapist_referrals. This website provides referrals to therapists who practice acceptance and commitment therapy (ACT).

Behavioral Tech: www.behavioraltech.org. This website provides referrals to therapists who specialize in dialectal behavior therapy (DBT).

Mindful Living Programs. www.mindfullivingprograms.com. Contact Mindful Living Programs for information about online or phone counseling.

Mindfulness-Based Cognitive Therapy (MBCT). www.mbct.com. You can also search the Internet for "mindfulness-based cognitive therapy" for further resources.

references

American Psychiatric Association. 1994. *Diagnostic and Statistical Manual of Mental Disorders.* 4th ed., text revision. Washington, DC: American Psychiatric Association.

Barlow, D. H. 2002. *Anxiety and Its Disorders: The Nature and Treatment of Anxiety and Panic.* 2nd ed. New York: Guilford Press.

Benson, H. 1993. The relaxation response. In *Mind Body Medicine,* edited by D. Goleman and J. Gurin. New York: Consumer Reports Books.

Brach, T. 2004. *Radical Acceptance: Embracing Your Life with the Heart of a Buddha.* New York: Bantam Books.

Brantley, J. 2007. *Calming Your Anxious Mind.* Oakland, CA: New Harbinger.

Center for Mindfulness. 2008. Research. www.umassmed.edu/Content. aspx?id=42066.

Davidson, R. J. 2006. Transforming the Mind: Perspectives from Affective Neuroscience. Keynote address at the fourth annual scientific conference: Investigating and Integrating Mindfulness in Medicine, Health Care, and Society, Worcester, MA.

Davidson, R. J., J. Kabat-Zinn, J. Schumacher, M. Rosenkranz, D. Muller, S. F. Santorelli, F. Urbanowski, A. Harrington, K. Bonus, and J. F. Sheridan. 2003. Alterations in brain and immune function produced by mindfulness meditation. *Psychosomatic Medicine* 65(4):564-570.

Davidson, R. J. 2009. Keynote address at the seventh annual scientific conference: Investigating and Integrating Mindfulness into Medicine, Health Care, and the Larger Society, Worcester, MA.

Einstein, A. 1996. *Bite-Size Einstein: Quotations on Just About Everything from the Greatest Mind of the Twentieth Century.* New York: Macmillan.

Ekman, P., and R. J. Davidson. 1995. *The Nature of Emotion: Fundamental Questions.* New York: Oxford University Press.

Frankl, V. E. 2000. *Man's Search for Meaning.* Boston: Beacon Press.

Goldin, P. 2008. The Matrix of Mindfulness. Presentation at the sixth annual scientific conference: Investigating and Integrating Mindfulness-Based Interventions into Medicine, Health Care, and the Larger Society, Worcester, MA.

Goldin, P. 2009. Neural Bases of Mindfulness Meditation, Emotional Reactivity, and Regulation in Individuals with Social Anxiety Disorder. Presentation at the seventh annual scientific conference: Investigating and Integrating Mindfulness-Based Interventions into Medicine, Health Care, and the Larger Society, Worcester, MA.

Goleman, D. 2003. *Destructive Emotions: How Can We Overcome Them?* New York: Bantam.

Gross, J. J., and R. W. Levenson. 1997. Hiding feelings: The acute effects of inhibiting negative and positive emotion. *Journal of Abnormal Psychology* 106(1):95-103.

Henderson, L. 2002. *Social Fitness Client Manual.* Palo Alto, CA: Henderson.

Henderson, L. 2009. Telephone conversation. January 12, 2009.

Henderson, L., and P. G. Zimbardo. 1998. Shyness. In *Encyclopedia of Mental Health*, edited by R. Schwarzer, R. Cohen Silver, D. Spiegel, N. E. Adler, R. D. Parke, C. Peterson, and H. Friedman. San Diego: Academic Press.

Henderson, L., and P. G. Zimbardo. 2001. Shyness as a clinical condition: The Stanford Model. In *International Handbook of Social Anxiety*, edited by L. Alden and R. Crozier. Sussex, England: John Wiley and Sons.

Henderson, L., P. G. Zimbardo, and B. J. Carducci. 2001. Shyness. In *The Corsini Encyclopedia of Psychology and Behavioral Science*, edited by W. E. Craighead and C. B. Nemeroff. New York: John Wiley and Sons.

Joyce, J. 2006. *Dubliners.* Clayton, DE: Prestwick House.

Kabat-Zinn, J. 1982. An outpatient program in behavioral medicine for chronic pain patients based on the practice of mindfulness meditation: Theoretical considerations and preliminary results. *General Hospital Psychiatry* 4(1):33-47.

Kabat-Zinn, J., M. D. Massion, J. L. Kristeller, L. G. Peterson, K. E. Fletcher, L. Pbert, W. R. Lenderking, and S. F. Santorelli. 1992. Effectiveness of a meditation-based program in the treatment of anxiety disorders. *American Journal of Psychiatry* 149(7):936-943.

Kagan, J. 1994. *Galen's Prophecy: Temperament in Human Nature.* New York: Basic Books.

Katie, B., with S. Mitchell. 2002. *Loving What Is: Four Questions That Can Change Your Life.* New York: Random House.

Kornfield, J. 1993. *A Path with Heart.* New York: Bantam Books.

Kornfield, J. 2007. Comments at the conference The Wise Heart and the Mindful Brain, R. Cassidy Seminars, San Francisco, CA.

Kramer, G. 2008. *Insight Dialogue: The Interpersonal Path to Freedom.* Boston: Shambhala.

Linehan, M. M. 1993. *Skills Training Manual for Treating Borderline Personality Disorder.* New York: Guilford Press.

Miller, J., K. Fletcher, and J. Kabat-Zinn. 1995. Three-year follow-up and clinical implications of a mindfulness meditation-based stress reduction intervention in the treatment of anxiety disorders. *General Hospital Psychiatry* 17(3):192-200.

Neff, K. 2007. A comparison of self-compassion and present moment awareness as they relate to positive psychological functioning. Presentation at the fifth annual scientific conference: Investigating and Integrating Mindfulness in Medicine, Health Care, and Society, Worcester, MA.

Nhat Hahn, T. 2001. *Anger: Wisdom for Cooling the Flames.* New York: Berkley Publishing.

Orsillo, S. M., and L. Roemer, eds. 2005. *Acceptance and Mindfulness-Based Approaches to Anxiety: Conceptualization and Treatment.* New York: Springer.

Pattakos, A. 2008. *Prisoners of Our Thoughts: Viktor Frankl's Principles for Discovering Meaning in Life and Work.* San Francisco: Berrett-Koehler.

Pert, C. 1998. *Molecules of Emotion: The Science Behind Mind-Body Medicine.* New York: Simon and Schuster.

Purdon, C. 1999. Thought suppression and psychopathology. *Behaviour Research and Therapy* 37(11):1029-1054.

Rumi. 1995. *The Essential Rumi.* Translated by Coleman Barks. San Francisco: Harper.

Scheick, W. J. 2002. Reader's forum. *Parabola* 27(3): 124-125.

Schore, A. N. 2003. *Affect Dysregulation and Disorders of the Self* [and] *Affect Regulation and the Repair of the Self.* 2 vols. New York: W. W. Norton.

Segal, Z., M. Williams, and J. Teasdale. 2002. *Mindfulness-Based Cognitive Therapy for Depression.* New York: Guilford Press.

Seneca, L. A. 1969. *Letters from a Stoic.* London: Penguin Classics.

Siegel, D. 2007a. Comments at the conference The Wise Heart and the Mindful Brain, R. Cassidy Seminars, San Francisco, CA.

Siegel, D. 2007b. *The Mindful Brain: Reflections and Attunement in the Cultivation of Well-Being.* New York: W. W. Norton and Company.

Siegel, D. 2007c. An Interpersonal Neurobiology of Psychotherapy: Relationships, the Brain, and the Development of Well-Being. Post-conference institute at the twenty-sixth annual UC Davis National Child Abuse and Neglect Conference, Sacramento, CA.

Stone, H., and S. Stone. 1998. *Embracing Ourselves: The Voice Dialogue Manual.* Novato, CA: Nataraj Publishing.

Teasdale, J. D., Z. Segal, and J. M. Williams. 1995. How does cognitive therapy prevent relapse and why should attentional control (mindfulness) training help? *Behaviour Research and Therapy* 33(1):25-39.

Tolle, E. 2004. *The Power of Now.* Novato, CA: New World Library.

Walcott, D. 1976. *Sea Grapes.* London: Cape.

Wallenchinsky, D., and A. Wallace. 2005. *The New Book of Lists: The Original Compendium of Curious Information.* New York: Canongate.

Williams, M. G., J. Teasdale, Z. Segal, and J. Kabat-Zinn. 2007. *The Mindful Way Through Depression: Freeing Yourself from Chronic Unhappiness.* New York: Guilford Press.

Steve Flowers, MFT, conducts mindfulness-based stress reduction online programs and is the founder and director of the mindfulness-based stress reduction clinic at Enloe Medical Center in Chico, CA. He also works in private practice as a psychotherapist.

Foreword writer Jeffrey Brantley, MD, is a consulting associate in the Duke Department of Psychiatry and the founder and director of the Mindfulness-Based Stress Reduction Program at Duke University's Center for Integrative Medicine. He is author of *Calming Your Anxious Mind*.

The Mindful Path Through Shyness Program

Participating in Steve Flowers' eight-week Mindful Path Through Shyness Program can greatly help you on your personal path through shyness and social anxiety. The program and its accompanying workbook are free and can be downloaded from www.mindfullivingprograms.com. Also available at the website are audio/visual recordings to assist you in your meditation practice, an online Mindful Path Through Shyness Forum, and information about Flowers' eight-week online class.